Optimize Yourself

Optimize Yourself

'To be the BEST you can be'

Martin Robert Hall

AuthorHouse™
1663 Liberty Drive
Bloomington, IN 47403
www.authorhouse.com
Phone: 1-800-839-8640

© 2011 by Martin Robert Hall. All rights reserved.

No part of this book may be reproduced, stored in a retrieval system, or transmitted by any means without the written permission of the author.

First published by AuthorHouse   09/15/2011

ISBN: 978-1-4670-0001-7 (sc)
ISBN: 978-1-4670-0002-4 (ebk)

Printed in the United States of America

Any people depicted in stock imagery provided by Thinkstock are models, and such images are being used for illustrative purposes only.
Certain stock imagery © Thinkstock.

Because of the dynamic nature of the Internet, any web addresses or links contained in this book may have changed since publication and may no longer be valid. The views expressed in this work are solely those of the author and do not necessarily reflect the views of the publisher, and the publisher hereby disclaims any responsibility for them.

Spreading the love

To my family and friends and everybody who has supported me on my journey to become an author. This is a dream come true for me and I would like to acknowledge some of you who have made a significant contribution.

To my best friend Scott for being there right from the beginning of this journey, I hope you are holding this book in your hands right now with a smile on your face. You always believed in me and are a major part of why this book exists. I love you man.

To Mark, another great friend of mine. Thank you for the amazing artwork you have provided me with throughout this journey and for the creation of the 'caricature'. I remember the night when you first sketched him (or me) as we sat enjoying a cold beer!

To my family, you know who you are. Mum, Dad, Bro, Sis. You have all supported me on this journey in your own ways but ultimately it all comes down to love. Thank you for always encouraging me to do whatever I have wanted in my life, I have never felt any pressure to be anything other than who I want to be and that alone is an amazing thing to say. I am now living my dreams and ultimately it is down to you.

To all my friends in business (Innospacer's) who have in your own ways kept the positive momentum flowing at all times and ultimately made the journey that much more enjoyable—Danny, Malcolm, James, Ben, Bradley—thanks for "bbbbrrrriiinnnGGGiiin IT" each day! Happy times.

Martin Robert Hall

To all of my clients who have invested your money, confidence and trust in me to support you to be the best you can be. I have thoroughly enjoyed working with you all and the learning I have gained from this experience forms a major part of this book.

AND finally, thank you to you the reader for purchasing this book. I hope it fulfils your expectations and sets you on a path of excellence for the rest of your days.

Contents

About the author .... *xi*
Introduction .... *xii*
Potential Unlimited *1*

Optimal Response *3*

Success is promised to nobody *6*

Response-ability *10*

It's a crash course *11*

The four pillars of success *12*

The Binding Ingredient *19*

Open Wide *22*

Ignite Your Imagination *23*

From Imagination to Realisation *32*

Access all areas *35*

Synchronize effort with outcome *36*

Success Mapping *39*

Quantum Leaping 41

Limitation Disengage 44

Making friends with fear 48

Your Operating Zone 51

Three enemies to success 52

Success filters 58

Results Guaranteed 61

Optimal Performance 66

Pick your own team 67

Re-condition yourself 70

Optimize your inner genius 75

Fuel your performance 77

Minimal Effort—Maximum Results 91

Make a pledge 94

Positive Reinforcement 97

Optimize Your Mindset 98

Time for Reflection 105

Start the day with a bang 108

Bringing it all together 109

Just Do It 112
Success Formula 114
On your marks, get set 114
Bridge the Gap 117
Potential Unlimited Exercises 118
Open Wide Exercises 120
Limitation Disengage Exercises 125
Optimal Performance 127
Exercises and strategies 127
My closing comments 140
Recommended Reading 142
Optimize Yourself Workshops 148

About the author

Martin Robert Hall is a performance specialist who runs his own consultancy and training business which specialises in helping individuals, teams and organisations to be the best they can be.

Martin has studied human excellence for over 10 years and takes the principles used by the World's greatest achievers in both sport and business and shows you how to adopt the same principles in your life to tap into your unique potential and achieve what you are truly capable of.

He has worked with a wide range of people including professional athletes, students, sales executives and business owners and showed them how to adopt these principles into their lives to achieve greater levels of success.

Martin has a global vision that includes making a positive difference to millions of lives around the world. He is highly passionate, bursting with energy, slightly wacky (!) and has a very enthusiastic and engaging approach to his work. He's very down to earth and always cracking a laugh and a smile.

If you are interested in working with Martin please contact him at:
www.martinroberthall.com

"In life there are no accidents, everything comes as a result of the law of cause and effect. The question is: Are you going to be a cause in the world or at the effect of the world?"

Introduction

Hello and thank you for taking the time to read my book. This book is a dream of mine and I am extremely pleased to have this opportunity to share my insights with you.

From a very young age I have always been fascinated with people and believe that we each have the potential to achieve extraordinary things in our lifetime. I have dedicated much of my life to understanding how to maximise this potential and this book is a celebration of that and a reflection of all my learning's.

One of the most important distinctions I have made in my life is that success does not happen by accident—never. There are certain principles that successful people apply in their lives that can be applied by us all and we can go on to achieve the same or greater levels of success if we wish. The key lies in identifying these principles and then understanding how to apply them most effectively in our lives.

I will make you the sincere promise that if you apply the principles inside, you will not only achieve more success in your life but also reach your goals much faster than ever before.

Statistics show that only 10% of people actually get past the first chapter of books they start reading. A startling statistic I think you will agree but even more so because it is a reflection of how many people fail to finish what they start. Now of course I know you are not in the 90% majority so I thought I would take the earliest opportunity to congratulate you on finishing this book!

I remember when I first started reading books on Personal Achievement, before that point I thought that I hated reading and only briefly read magazines that were of interest to me. I associated reading with long, boring and confusing texts that they had you read at school! I would glance over a book and the thought of reading it either bored me or scared me to be honest so I told myself that reading wasn't for me. What a load of nonsense! It was just that the books I had been made to read were of no real interest to me.

As soon as I started reading books that added value to my life and helped me to achieve what I wanted, I became an avid reader.

Benjamin Franklin, one of the greatest leaders in history, once said that man can either buy his wisdom or borrow it. By buying it, he pays full price in personal time and treasure. But by borrowing it, he capitalizes on the lessons learned from the failure of others.

This book is an opportunity to avoid paying the full price and borrow the lessons from some of the greatest achievers of all time.

Whatever your own goals are in life, this book will help you to achieve them much faster and easier by applying the principles I share with you. The principles have worked for the thousands of successful people from all of history. I have applied many of them in my own life, I am still mastering some of them and I have shared many of them to great effect in my work with a wide range of people, from school kids to business leaders to professional athletes.

You may already be incredibly successful and a part of you might think that I can't teach you anything new but I know that no matter how successful you already are in your life, you can always improve and become better.

I believe that is what life is all about and this book is a celebration of that potential and more importantly, how to maximise it.

I encourage you to approach this book with an open mind, eager to learn new ways of reaching your goals faster and enjoying more success in your life.

Structured for Optimal Experience

The book has been structured specifically for optimal learning and application. I have broken the book down into a precise order where each chapter follows from one to the next purposely to allow optimal learning and effective application of the principles.

Firstly I will share with you the insights and philosophies of great achievers and then specifically how you can adopt these principles in your own life. The book has been designed for you to read it from front to back, first opening your mind to the principles which are backed up with examples and stories of great achievers, followed by step by step instructions on how to apply these principles yourself.

There are a range of exercises at the end of the book that will help bridge the gap between learning and application of the principles. After all, the book is all about maximising your performance and that cannot be achieved without action. You can complete the exercises all at once when you have read through the book or complete them as you go. It is entirely up to you. I have organised it this way because we all have different approaches to learning and this method will allow you to choose what works best for you.

Getting the most out of this book

One thing I highly recommend while you are reading is to have a pen or pencil handy and highlight or note down anything that resonates with you. This is a method recommended by many authors and I can confirm that it really helps to heighten your learning experience.

And don't just read the book once and then leave it to collect dust on your shelf! Remember that repetition is the most simple and proven method for learning, it always has been and always will be. Dip into the book regularly, remind yourself of the principles and integrate them into your life.

And just like I heard author and professional speaker Nigel Risner once say, if you read it twice and you like it then don't lend it to a friend, buy them a copy instead and then you will be helping me out too!

Okay, that is enough build up, it's time to ROCK this show, get comfortable, grab your pen and let's get cracking . . .

Chapter 1

Potential Unlimited

Don't accept a life of mediocrity when you hold such infinite potential within the fortress of your mind. Dare to tap into your greatness, it's your birthright".

Robin Sharma

—Voted #2 Leadership Guru in the World—

When I was growing up, one of the comments I heard repeated time and again was "he has the potential". I heard it said many times about myself and about many other kids from teachers, coaches and parents mostly. You may recall hearing it said about yourself on many occasions too. The problem was in the words that followed, which for the majority of the time started with the ever so timely "but".

Then followed all the reasons why that potential was not being fulfilled. This triggered a deep curiosity within me about what potential was, why some people seem to utilise more of it than others and more importantly how they did it.

One clear distinction I made early on was that all great achievers seemed to have one thing in common and this was what I class as a 'winning mindset'. I have studied lots of successful people from all walks of life and learnt that the most successful people all share similar outlooks and philosophies on success and achievement.

The more I learnt, the more I understood that success is not an accident. Success is a series of steps, it is a process and it can be broken down and applied by anybody.

"Success leaves clues"

Anthony Robbins

—Peak Performance Coach and Bestselling Author—

Each person is unique in their ability to tap into their potential. Some people learn how to harness their potential from a young age, some learn later in life and many never learn how to at all. A lot of it depends on your upbringing and what you learnt in the first 7 years of your life. This period is known as the 'imprint period' and it is when we form most of our beliefs and attitudes.

I talk more about this in a later chapter but for now I want to focus on what I believe is the single most important factor in personal achievement, something that you have full control over rather than something that happened in the past or when you were growing up. Something that will do more to determine how successful you become than all of the other insights, lessons and strategies you will ever learn on success and achievement.

Optimal Response

What you expect from life you will very often get, whether it is what you really want or not.

> "Successful people come in all sizes, shapes, ages, and colours and they have widely varying degrees of intelligence and education. But they have one thing in common: They expect more good out of life than bad. They expect success more often than failure. And they do succeed".
>
> **Earl Nightingale**

Much of your success in life comes down to your attitude. How you respond to the events of life greatly determines how successful you become.

Much of what happens in our lives is out of our control. The only thing we really have control over is our thoughts and our actions and how we respond to the events we experience in life. We have little control over the weather, the economy, the traffic, other people—the only thing we really have control over is ourselves and how we respond to these events.

That response is your choice.

The longer I live, the more I realize the impact of attitude on life. Attitude to me is more important than facts, it is more important than the past, the education, the money, than circumstances, than failure, than successes, than what other people think or say or do. It is more important than appearance, giftedness or skill. It will make or break a company . . . a church . . . a home. The remarkable thing is we have a choice every day regarding the attitude we will embrace for that day. We cannot change our past . . . we cannot change the fact that people will act in a certain way. We cannot change the inevitable. The only thing we can do is play on the one string we have, and that is our attitude. I am convinced that life is 10% what happens to me and 90% of how I react to it. And so it is with you . . . we are in charge of our attitudes".

Charles R Swindoll

Your attitude determines how you respond to the events in your life. In psychology terms this is referred to as your 'locus of control'. If you have an internal locus of control then you accept that it is you who is in control of your thoughts and actions. If you have an external locus of control then you blame external circumstances that are outside of your control.

Successful people have an internal locus of control. They accept that they are responsible for the way their life turns out. They realise that it is no good focusing on and blaming things outside their control and they respond to life in a way that serves them and accelerates them towards their goals.

They do their best to control what they actually have control over and they let go of the rest. They do not waste their time trying to control things they have no control over. Instead they focus all their energy on controlling their own thoughts and actions, knowing that the right responses will lead them to the best results.

Reflection

One of my childhood heroes was Michael Jordan, the famous basketball player and regarded as the greatest player of all time. He literally broke every record there was to break in basketball and won every personal accolade too. He won two Olympic gold medals and what he did for the sport of basketball was nothing short of phenomenal. What was most impressive about his career though was his attitude to the game.

It didn't all start out as easy as you might think for Michael Jordan. He actually failed to make his school basketball team which for many kids would have derailed them and put them off. However Jordan's response was to prove the coach wrong for not picking him. He started working harder than ever before, putting in hours and hours of practice.

> His sports instructor was one of the first to notice the change and said this: "Usually I arrive at school between 07.00 am and 07.30 am, Michael was there before me. Each time I came in and opened the door, I heard the sound of the ball bouncing, in autumn, in winter, in summer. Almost every morning I had to ask him to leave the court".
>
> He continued with this approach throughout his career and was known for being one of the hardest trainers ever. He always applied himself fully; it was no accident that he became as good as he did. He was not afraid to make mistakes and to put himself on the line. He was not afraid to fail either, he accepted it as part of the process of improvement: "I can accept failure, everyone fails at something. But I can't accept not trying
>
> He was constantly quoted repeating similar things on the topic of failure and responding in the best possible way. He had a hugely competitive streak and strived to be the best until eventually he became the best, the best of all time.
>
> It was his response to the disappointments and setbacks in his career that made him as successful as he was. Without this one single quality he wouldn't have become nearly as successful as he did, in fact he wouldn't have even made his school team! I think it is fair to say he grasped the concept of 'optimal response'.

It is possible to achieve great things as many people have done time and time again but essentially the only person who can control how you respond to the events in your life is YOU.

Success is promised to nobody

I believe there are no limits on the amount of success you can achieve in your lifetime but by no means is it promised to anybody.

One thing I believe any successful person who ever achieved anything worthwhile has understood is the principle of applying themselves. All successful people believe in giving their best—applying themselves fully. It is by giving their all that they continually improve and eventually achieve incredible success.

Look at Michael Jordan for example—rejected by his high school team, he responded by applying himself more than before, he worked harder than any other player and eventually he made the team and quickly became their best player. He continued to give his best at all times and as a result he kept on improving, eventually becoming the best player the world has ever seen. He didn't start out as the best, far from it. What he did do was he worked harder than most by continuously giving his best and as a result his progress was astonishing.

Was he more talented than the other players?

Was he born with the ability to play basketball?

Was he born to be a great basketball player?

Of course he wasn't. He just practised more than everybody else. When he got told he wasn't good enough he worked harder to make sure he became good enough.

What about Tiger Woods? Was he born to be the greatest golfer of his time? Or anybody else who has become great at anything in their lives, is it God given talent or is it consistent practice that makes the difference?

Did you know that by the time Tiger Woods was nine years old he had played more rounds of golf than most full time professionals had?!

What about Bruce Lee? Widely considered the most influential martial artist of the 20th century, he practised for hours on end every single day, sometimes practising the same kick over 1000 times.

There is a benchmark that has been calculated from studying Olympic athletes, chess grandmasters and world class musicians that predicts that all the greatest performers in each field have put in 10,000 hours worth of practise to reach the top level.

As I said, 'success is not an accident'. Whether we are talking about The Beatles who played for eight hours per day, seven days per week at a strip club in Germany before they became famous or we are talking about a young Michael Jordan who was on the basketball court practising every day before school even opened—the reason they became the best is because they applied themselves and put in the practise.

It wasn't because they were more talented than the rest, or because they were born with a gift. It is because they applied themselves more than anybody else.

It is this attitude, this approach to life that great achievers have running through their veins—to give their best all the time.

Ironically, by not doing it just for the results they achieve and by doing their best just for the sake of giving their all, they keep on improving and so do their results. The results (often spectacular) are just a by-product of giving their best.

> *"If anything is worth doing—it is worth doing your best"*
>
> **George Leonard**
>
> —Bestselling author and leader on human potential—

I remember going along to watch an academy of footballers who had been released by professional clubs once. The academy had been built to offer those talented footballers who had slipped through the net another opportunity for a professional football career. The coach came over about half way through the training session to ask my thoughts and I distinctly remember telling him that it was no surprise most of them had been released by their clubs—their attitude was extremely poor. I remember thinking that many of them would not even get a game at my amateur club! Not because of their ability but because they simply didn't apply themselves. Obviously they had the ability as they had been at a professional club for several years but ability alone is not enough and boy did it show. If only they had responded to their disappointment of being released by working harder to improve themselves, many of them might have got another chance but instead it was clear that many of them had just given up.

I don't know about you but I certainly know that I always feel better about myself when I am giving my all and fully applying myself to something. It doesn't matter what it is and it doesn't matter how well I am doing in comparison to anyone or anything, as long as I am trying and giving what I am capable of there and then, in that moment. I feel much better about myself, my confidence goes up a notch and I can handle disappointments and setbacks easier. I am happier for other people and their success. I feel more satisfied, fulfilled and genuinely happy when I have applied myself fully at anything.

And I believe it is when we give less than we are capable of that these feelings evaporate. It seems that I am not the only one either;

Music producer, entrepreneur and author Russell Simmons, who has been described as one of the most innovative and influential figures in modern American business and culture has this to say on the topic;

"The pain that's created by avoiding hard work is actually much worse than any pain created from the actual work itself. Because if you don't begin to work on those ideas that God has blessed you with, they will become stagnant inside of you and eventually begin to eat away at you. You might seem OK on the outside, but inside you will be ill from not getting those ideas out of your heart and into the world. Stalling leads to sickness. But taking steps, even baby steps, always leads to success."

George Leonard, life-long teacher on human potential and author of the book *Mastery* says;

"Much of the world's depression and discontent . . . can ultimately be traced to our unused energy, our untapped potential."

And if that is not enough to convince you, then you can go all the way back to quote Jesus who said;

"If you bring forth what is inside you, what you bring forth will save you. If you don't bring forth what is inside you, what you don't bring forth will destroy you."

So it is clear that it is not just me who feels this way about feeling great when I try my best. It is a philosophy which is maintained from great achievers many thousands of years ago right up until the present day.

Response-ability

So do you see how your success is in your own hands? You are not guaranteed success in life—it comes as a result of applying yourself fully and making the right choices.

It is your ability to respond to the events of life that will determine much of your success.

So how would you rate your response-ability these days?

Do you expect good things to happen to you? Do you accept that your life to date is a sum of all the choices you have made? Do you accept that if you want to lead a successful life then it is up to you and only you?

Or:

Do you blame others for your circumstances? Do you moan and complain about all the things that happen to you? Do you make excuses and constantly dwell on things?

Either way it's your choice.

You either choose to be a victim of life or a creator of life. The choice is yours—It always will be.

It's a crash course

Do you accept what life throws at you or do you respond with a tenacity and determination to achieve what you want?

Successful people know that things will not go in their favour all the time, in fact much of the time things do not go to plan and this is when many people give up. Understanding that setbacks, disappointments and obstacles are all part of the process is crucial to keeping positive and heading in the right direction.

Unfortunately many people turn back as soon as they come up against a road block. The trouble with responding like this is you can quickly develop a habit for turning back, giving up and avoiding many of life's challenges. The more you do this, the more you end up avoiding and before you know it you are running away from life instead of running towards it.

Successful people develop a resilience for life's challenges. They know it is natural to come up against obstacles, they accept them and even look forward to them at times because it makes the end result that bit more satisfying. If it was all plain sailing then surely it would be boring!

I know I have come up against many obstacles so far in writing this book. I have written the whole book, ripped it up and started again. I have had mental blocks, doubts, changed my mind on many things but I am determined to finish it no matter how many challenges I face and when I do it will be even more satisfying.

> *"Success is going from one disaster to another without any loss of enthusiasm"*
>
> **Winston Churchill**

Because successful people understand that obstacles and setbacks are all part of the process, they are better prepared for when they arrive. By no means do they look for them to show up but when they do, they are not deterred by them. They just accept them and look for the best possible solution around them.

How do you respond when you come up against life's challenges?

Understanding that your response is within your control and that it is the most powerful tool in your armoury is crucial to your success.

The four pillars of success

There are many attributes that make up a winning attitude and they are all important but there are four key ones which I believe will help you achieve success much faster than any of the rest. I call these the Four Pillars of Success, they are:

Persistence

> *"Nothing in the world can take the place of persistence. Talent will not; nothing is more common than unsuccessful men with talent. Genius will not;*

unrewarded genius is almost a proverb. Education will not; the world is full of educated derelicts. Persistence and determination are omnipotent. The slogan 'press on' has solved and always will solve the problems of the human race."

Calvin Coolidge

Persistence is the ability to keep trying, keep working hard and to never, ever give up. All great achievers know that persistence is essential to success and they practise it by simply refusing to give up.

Persistent people bounce back from disappointments and setbacks. They look for other ways to achieve what they want when their plans don't work. They do not let external circumstances stop them. They understand that it is their choice to keep on fighting and that is what they do. They find another way, another solution and they continue to persist until they succeed.

"If the first plan which you adopt does not work successfully, replace it with a new plan; if this new plan fails to work, replace it in turn with still another, and so on, until you find a plan which does work. Right here is the point at which the majority of men meet with failure, because of their lack of

persistence in creating new plans to take the place of those which fail."

Napoleon Hill

Successful people don't give up just because the going gets tough. They know it is not always going to be smooth sailing and they will face challenges, setbacks and disappointments but that is just part of the journey. It certainly does not mean you give in.

When you think about it, if you simply refuse to give up then you actually have to succeed! The only time you will fail is when you fail to keep trying.

Make persistence a part of your life and you will surely become a success.

Optimism

"The most readily identifiable quality of a total winner is an attitude of personal optimism and enthusiasm"

Dr Denis Waitley

—Bestselling author and consultant on human performance—

Optimism is the ability to stay focused on the prize when everything seems to be going against you. It is a critical component of successful people and closely related to your ability to be persistent.

If you are not optimistic about your plans and actions then you will most likely give up before you succeed. When you approach things with an optimistic attitude, you persist in the face of difficulty, you find solutions to problems and you make progress quicker and easier just by expecting to succeed.

If you are not looking for the good in a situation, how are you going to find it?!

I read this story by Debbie Ford which I think exemplifies an attitude of optimism perfectly:

"One day, twin boys went off with their grandfather on an outing. They walked through the woods until they came upon an old barn. When the boys and their grandfather stepped inside to explore, one of the boys immediately started complaining: 'Grampa, let's get out of here. The old barn stinks like horse manure.' The boy stood near the door, angry because he now had manure on his new shoes. Before the old man could respond he saw his other grandson running happily through the barn's many stalls. 'What are you looking for?' he asked the second little boy. 'Why are you so happy?' The boy looked up and said, 'With all that horse manure in here there must be a pony somewhere.'"

The opposite of an optimist is a pessimist. A pessimist will always find something to go wrong because they are constantly looking for it—they will always be facing problems and challenges because it is what they expect to find. An optimist on the other hand looks for the good in each situation and as a result they experience more positive results. When they do face a problem or a challenge, they remain optimistic and find the solution much quicker.

> *"The pessimist sees difficulty in every opportunity. The optimist sees the opportunity in every difficulty"*
>
> **Winston Churchill**

Optimists find the achievement of their goals much easier and more enjoyable simply because that is what they expect. Pessimists find it much harder to achieve what they want and as a result are much more likely to give up.

Give yourself a greater chance of success and commit to approaching your life with an optimistic attitude.

Constantly Raise your Game

"Excellence is the gradual result of always striving to do better"

Pat Riley

It does not matter where your starting point is or how far you are away from achieving your goals as long as you commit to continuous improvement. If you do then you will not only achieve your goals—you will exceed them.

Most people see their goals as impossible because they seem so far away. They don't know how they will ever get there and this often stops them even starting. If only they would start from where they are and keep improving bit by bit, they would eventually surpass many of their own expectations.

I learnt on a performance coaching course that the most common time people give up on their goals is before the very first step. I believe this is because they cannot see how they are going to achieve their goals and as a result they don't even start. Well remember that for every great achievement ever recorded, that person started off at some point below where you are right now. They had less knowledge, less skill and less ability at some point on their journey as you do right now. But by committing to constant and never ending improvement, they continued to improve until they achieved what they wanted.

Great achievers are always trying to improve. The best in every field are not competing against anybody else but themselves. They have high standards and are continuously pushing their boundaries, trying to improve on their last effort.

Michael Phelps, world class swimmer and the most decorated Olympian of all time said that his Coach has always instilled in him this notion;

'The great champions—there is nobody on their level and so when they are competing, they're competing against themselves and only themselves.'

Successful people apply the principle of applying themselves fully, not for the sake of being better than others but for being the 'best they can be'.

"Yes there are times when the Gold medal only goes to the winner. But not in the race of life, where the winners are those who are superior not to others but to their former selves"

Robert K Cooper

—Highly Respected Author and Leadership Expert —

When I was studying exercise physiology I learnt that your muscles grow by the principle of 'progressive overload'. This means that the only way to keep getting bigger and stronger muscles is by consistently lifting heavier weights. If you keep lifting the same weights, your muscles will stay the same size and strength. You have to keep increasing the weight, even if the increase is tiny.

It is the same with anything that you want to make progress in. As long as you commit to constant and never ending improvement, you will keep progressing.

So where do you need to apply this principle in your life? In everything I say!

Just imagine how great your life would be in a few years if you made a commitment to constant and never ending improvement?

Remember that it does not matter where you start and how you start, as long as you start and improve little by little each time. There is no need to feel overwhelmed by any task, no matter how big it is, as long as you start by doing something and keep doing a bit more than last time.

Life is all about continuous growth and improvement. Commit to constantly raising your game and eventually your game will be untouchable!

Enthusiasm

"Enthusiasm is one of the most powerful engines of success. When you do a thing, do it with all your might. Put your whole soul into it. Stamp it with your own personality. Be active, be energetic, be enthusiastic and faithful, and you will accomplish your object. Nothing great was ever achieved without enthusiasm."

Ralph Waldo Emerson

—Successful author, poet and philosopher—

Think about someone you know that has a natural enthusiasm for life. Now think about how they make you feel when you are around them.

Successful people have enthusiasm in bucket loads, they are excited about life and about the things they are working towards. They are infectious and rub off on you when you are around them. Sometimes there is no better feeling than being around somebody that has enthusiasm.

All of the people I remember most positively in my life have enthusiasm. From teachers, coaches and bosses I have had to people I have met on my travels, at university and even strangers I have met at events.

Nothing can replace enthusiasm. It is like a driving force of psychological energy that rubs off on everybody around you, it pushes you through challenges and obstacles on your way to victory and it is all within your control.

"Enthusiasm is contagious—and so is lack of it"

Dale Carnegie

On the flip side, there is nothing worse than being around people that have no enthusiasm! It has an enormous impact and you can just feel the lack of energy in the air.

If you want to be successful, to have a positive influence on others and reach your goals much faster then get enthusiastic about everything you're doing.

The Binding Ingredient

There is one binding ingredient which brings these four pillars of success together. Without this ingredient, adopting these attitudes in your life is impossible.

I am talking about discipline. Discipline is the act of doing something whether you feel like it or not. Practising these new attitudes in your life requires discipline because there will be times when you really don't feel like it and it is at these times when you need discipline to make sure you follow through.

"With self-discipline almost anything is possible"

Theodore Roosevelt

—Former US President-

When you lack discipline in your life you end up believing the stories and excuses you tell yourself for not following through and you end up suffering by holding yourself back from achieving what you want. But the more you practise discipline, the more control you have over your actions and the easier it becomes to follow through on the things that will most likely bring you success.

Closing Thought

If you were to overhear a conversation between two people you love and respect in your life and they were talking about you, what would you want to hear them say about you and your attitude in life?

Once you have answered this question, discipline yourself to practise these attitudes in your life on a daily basis.

"To live is so startling it leaves little time for anything else"

Emily Dickinson

—Famous American Poet—

What attitude are you going to start LIVING by?

Here is a poem which I adapted from a campaign by Sportswear giant Nike which I think sums up a winner's attitude and this chapter nicely:

> Yes to putting in the miles while the rest of the world is asleep,
>
> To doing what I want, when I want to do it,
>
> To pushing through the pain because giving up hurts more,
>
> Yes to not being afraid to fail,
>
> To doing it for the love, not the money,
>
> To doing it for myself, my friends and my loved ones,
>
> Yes to speeding up as I pass you by,
>
> Yes to self-belief, knowing that I'm good but I can always be better,
>
> Yes to claiming my place, to challenging the rules. To playing my own game,
>
> No there isn't anything I cannot do,
>
> Yes to making myself heard,
>
> Yes to stepping up and saying
>
> 'Here I am'

"Go to Chapter 6 and complete the exercises on developing a winning attitude in your life"

Chapter 2

Open Wide

"In 3,300 studies of leadership, seeking the common qualities possessed by great leaders through the ages, researchers found that the one quality all the studies had in common was vision. Leaders have vision. Non-leaders do not. Leaders have a vision of a better future for themselves, their families, and their organizations. They can see an ideal future in advance. They then work to make it a reality in the present".

Brian Tracy

—World Leading Authority on Peak Performance—

Successful people in all walks of life always have a vision for what they want and a plan of how to achieve it. They have spent the time working out what excites them in their life, what makes them tick and then they design their life around achieving that vision.

Vision is defined as the act or power of anticipating that which will or may come to be. It is also defined as a vivid, imaginative conception or anticipation.

Notice the words anticipation, conception and imagination here?

That is because all of your ideas first start off in your imagination. This is where they are first created, in the creative workshop of your mind.

As the quote says at the top of the page, leaders can see an ideal future in advance of it actually happening. They use their imagination to think about what they want and then they get to work on creating it.

Ignite Your Imagination

The very first step is the creation of your vision. The creation starts by running inspiring thoughts and pictures through your mind, daring to think beyond the limits you have learned from others and become child like in your thinking.

"Imagination is more important than knowledge"

Einstein

Great achievers from all walks of life have had great visions. They think and believe big. They ignore the limits, the doubts, the common way of thinking and they believe they can achieve whatever they want.

They are not naive and do not believe it will be easy, but they certainly don't become successful by limiting themselves and thinking small.

David Schwartz, the author of the classic book *The Magic of Thinking Big* says:

"Think Big and you'll live big. You'll live big in happiness. You'll live big in accomplishment. Big in income. Big in friends. Big in respect... Start now, right now, to discover how to make your thinking make magic for you. Start out with this thought of the great philosopher Disraeli: 'Life is too short to be little.'"

In order to think big and achieve big, you have to suspend any limiting beliefs or doubts that come with conventional thinking. I like to think that we would not have been given an imagination that has no limits in its ability to create if it were impossible to then make that vision a reality. What would be the point?

And this is what great achievers do, they dare to dream. They are not held back by everyday conventional thinking. They allow their imaginations to run wild and create an exciting vision for their ideal future. A vision that genuinely gets them excited, that activates the energy inside them to be able to get to work on that vision and make it happen. Without this initial vision, they would not be able to create the excitement, the passion, the enthusiasm and the motivation to fulfil their ambitions and make it a reality rather than just a dream.

Sir Richard Branson, the famous billionaire entrepreneur and founder or Virgin Companies, is somebody who understands the importance of having a big and exciting vision. He stated early on that he wanted Virgin "to be as well known around the world as Coca-cola". He had a vision for the company, one which excited him. "We'd love to be involved with the creation of something very special, something quite large and something quite exciting" he said, showing that he was someone who clearly had vision. He understood the importance of having an exciting vision, for

Virgin and for his life. When asked about retirement, he said "Because I don't see Virgin as a company but as a way of life and I fully enjoy it, I don't think I'll ever retire. His vision expands far beyond just a few years, but to the extent of his entire life. Maybe that's why he looks so damn good at his age!

Steve Jobs, Founder of technology giant Apple, is also another person who has great vision—"I want to put a dent in the universe" he said. I think you will agree that he is fulfilling that vision with revolutionary products such as the iPod, Apple Mac computers and the ever growing popular iPhone. He knew the importance of having a vision and also giving his best to achieve it. "Your work is going to fill a large part of your life and the only way to be truly satisfied is to do what you believe is great work". One of his top tips for success is to 'start small but think big'. Earlier in his career he was quoted saying "we started out to get a computer in the hands of everyday people, and we succeeded beyond our wildest dreams". Evidence of his belief in thinking big and starting small, and going on his success to date I wouldn't argue with that, would you?

Sir Alex Ferguson had his own unique vision when he became the manager of Manchester United FC in 1986. On his arrival at Old Trafford, he told the media "My greatest challenge is not what's happening at the moment, my greatest challenge was knocking Liverpool right off their f* *g perch"! Liverpool was the most successful football club in English football at the time when he took over and he envisioned taking Manchester United beyond that. He could see past the immediate present of the club being way behind Liverpool at the time when he arrived. At this time of writing (2010)—since Alex Ferguson took charge, Liverpool have won 2 league titles whilst Manchester United have won 11, equalling Liverpool's 18 league titles. He has therefore made massive progress towards his vision already and my guess is he will not fall short of surpassing it.

And just in case you are thinking that's fine, but you cannot relate to them because they are 'different from me' then think again. Richard Branson struggled with dyslexia during his younger years and dropped out of high school. Steve Jobs dropped out of college after just one term and travelled to India in search of spiritual enlightenment before he founded Apple. Sir Alex Ferguson's first job in football management was a part-time role and he was paid just £40 per week.

Every great achiever started off from a similar place to either where you are now or where you once were. It did not stop them having incredible vision and it should not stop you.

I remember listening to an audio programme by Dr Wayne Dyer who captured vision perfectly when he said:

> *The Wright brothers didn't contemplate the staying on the ground of things. Alexander Graham Bell didn't contemplate the non-communication of things. Thomas Edison didn't contemplate the darkness of things. In order to float an idea into your reality, you must be willing to do a somersault into the unconceivable and land on your feet, contemplating what you want instead of what you don't have."*

The final sentence in this quote is critical. Successful people think about what they want to create rather than what they don't have. I talked about optimism being one of the four pillars of success in the last chapter and the two go together. You have to focus on the positive aspects of what you want to create in the future and see what you want before it becomes a reality.

The average person has to see something before they believe it. Great achievers first see it in their minds and then create it for others to see and believe. This often takes courage.

It takes courage to go after what we really want in our lives. It takes boldness to state our ideas and stand by them regardless of what others think. We may get ridiculed, laughed at or even told that our ideas are crazy but great achievers accept that comes as part of thinking outside the box, outside the conventional way of thinking. People often may not agree with your ideas, they may not be able to see what you see but that does not mean that you shouldn't pursue them anyway.

One of my favourite programme's on TV is Dragon's Den. I love watching ambitious and hopeful entrepreneurs coming onto the show with a vision they are passionate about. Many of them have their ideas slammed, laughed at and told they will never work but it does not stop them from pursuing them just because of the opinion of others. Some of the ideas are crazy but that is what is great about the show! My favourite part of the show is when they revisit some of the entrepreneurs who failed to get investment and they find that they are doing really well. These entrepreneurs believed in their ideas regardless of what others told them and they pursued with them until they were successful. That takes courage.

Technology giant apple captured this perfectly in one of their adverts:

"Here's to the crazy ones. The misfits. The rebels. The trouble makers. The round pegs in the square holes. The ones who see things differently. They're not fond of rules and they have no respect for the status-quo. You can quote them, disagree with them, glorify, or vilify them. But the only thing you can't

do is ignore them. Because they change things. They push the human race forward. And while some may see them as the crazy ones, we see genius. Because the people who are crazy enough to think they can change the world, are the ones who do."

Your vision does not have to be world altering. Your vision just needs to capture the things that are important to you and the things that excite you. Your vision must be your own and it must reflect who you are and what you stand for. It shouldn't be different just for the sake of being different.

Reflection

Another person who I really admired when I was growing up was Arnold Schwarzenegger. As a skinny kid with a desire to grow some muscles, he was the most obvious role model for me. I started to read about him in magazines, listen to his advice on how to build such an impressive physique and the more I learnt about him, the more I understood there was much more to Arnold Schwarzenegger than just a huge slab of muscle!

He was somebody who really understood the importance of having vision and he seemed to have it from a very young age. At just 15 years old he declared:

"I want to be the best built man in the world. Then I want to go to America and be in movies. I want to be an actor".

Just 5 years later he became Mr Universe, otherwise known as The Greatest Bodybuilder on the planet. He remained at the top of the world of bodybuilding for many years and is widely regarded as the Greatest Bodybuilder of all time. He then went on to become a famous movie star. He achieved his vision that he stated at just 15 years old. Later he was quoted saying:

"All I know is that the first step is to create the vision, because when you see the vision there, the beautiful vision - that creates the 'want power.' For example, my wanting to be Mr. Universe came about because I saw myself so clearly, being up there on stage and winning."

He clearly had the ability to see his ideal future. He first created it in his mind and then he set about achieving it. He was not one to think small as I am sure you will agree.

He states that it was his vision that created his 'want power'. This gave him the desire, the motivation and the determination to work hard, to focus on his end goal and train extremely hard for many years to finally fulfil all of his ambitions.

When he was in America and at the peak of his bodybuilding career, he was taken aside and advised to invest his money wisely in a chain of gyms to secure his future once he retired from professional bodybuilding. His response was to laugh and instead he told the man that he was going to be a movie star and then become President of America.

Now that is what I call having belief in yourself! He did go on to become a movie star, one of the most famous action heroes of all time. And then in 2003 he made significant progress in politics when he became the Governor of California.

He has not yet achieved his goal of becoming President but he still has time even if it is a long shot!

As a teenager his idol was a bodybuilder named Reg Park. Arnold would collect pictures of him and constantly look at them and imagine himself being like his idol one day. Arnold said:

"The more I focused in on this image and worked and grew, the more I saw it was real and possible for me to be like him".

He constantly flooded his mind with images of him succeeding and achieving his ideal vision in the future. He used his vision to keep him motivated and focused until he achieved everything he set out to do and I am sure he is still doing it until this day.

Creating the vision first in his imagination and seeing it happening gave him the belief that it was possible.

> *He would seek out role models and think if it was possible for them then it was possible for him too. He did not believe in traditional modest thinking, he believed in thinking big and exciting things for himself and his future and as a result he achieved amazing things:*
>
> *"I knew I was a winner back in the late sixties. I knew I was destined for great things. People will say that kind of thinking is totally immodest. I agree. Modesty is not a word that applies to me in any way – I hope it never will".*

We all have the ability to use our imagination to the same extent as Arnold did and create a vision for our future that activates our 'want power' too. Unfortunately as we grow older and take on more and more responsibilities, our ability to visualise our ideal future becomes impaired by our day to day responsibilities such as paying the bills and all the other really exciting tasks we have to do! We allow our immediate responsibilities in our lives to cloud our ability to see past all of that and to imagine what we want our lives to be like in 3 to 5 years time.

If you allow what is happening in your immediate future to prevent you from seeing the long term bigger picture then you will forever be stuck in day to day living. You have to be able to see past your immediate future and imagine a future that would really excite you.

You have to suspend all of your limited thinking for the time being, see past the doubts and the reasons why it can't be done and create a vision for your future that stirs you up and gets you excited.

> *"The best performers ignore the odds, instead of limiting themselves to what's probable, the best will pursue the heart pounding, exciting, really big, difference*

making dreams—so long as achieving them might be possible"

Dr John Eliot

I am so often amazed by the amount of people who I meet who spend more time planning their weekly shopping lists or planning their summer holiday than they do planning their vision for their lives. They don't think to take the time to create a vision for their ideal future because they cannot immediately see how they would make it happen.

Just because you cannot immediately see how you would bring your vision to life is no reason to not create one in the first place. You cannot work out the 'how' until you have created the 'what'. The 'what' is always the very first step.

Without a vision for your life you just drift without any direction and purpose. You end up accepting what life throws at you because you have no pre determined alternative of your own. Having a vision for your life gives you a reason for getting out of bed in the morning, it puts a spring in your step and puts purpose behind everything you do.

People so often talk about lacking motivation. I don't think anybody lacks motivation, but people do lack having a vision that will motivate them.

From Imagination to Realisation

"Success is the progressive realisation of a worthy goal or ideal"

Earl Nightingale

There is a massive difference between being a dreamer and an achiever. We all have dreams and wishes for our life but doing something about them sets you apart from the average.

The bridge from your imagination to the realisation of your dreams is goals. All great achievers understand the importance of having goals. I like to think of goals as 'dreams with deadlines'.

If you don't put a deadline on your dreams then they will most likely just remain as dreams. When you set yourself a goal you are making a strong statement to the world that you are serious about living a successful life and not just a 'dreamer'.

There is a famous study which was carried out at the University of Harvard which focused on the power of goal setting. It was conducted on a group of graduates from Harvard's MBA program. In 1979 interviewers asked the question: 'Have you set clear, written goals for your future and made plans to accomplish them'?

The results of the questionnaire found that;

84% had no specific goals at all

13% had goals but they had not written them down

3% had clear written goals and plans to achieve them

10 years later, the interviewers once again interviewed the graduates of that class. They found;

The 13% of the class who had goals were on average earning twice as much as the 84% who had no goals at all.

And even more staggering—the 3% who had clear, written goals were earning on average, 10 times as much as the other 97% of the group put together,

Does that convince you of the power of having clear written goals in your life?

I hope so.

The great oil billionaire H. L. Hunt was once asked the secret of success. He replied that success requires two things;

1. Decide what you want.

Firstly you must know exactly what you want. Most people never make this decision.

2. You must decide the price you are willing to pay to achieve it and then pay that price.

This is a very simple and powerful formula to use when setting your goals. I believe that many people do not achieve what they want because they don't take the time to understand what will be required. They often approach their goals with false expectations and when the going gets tough or they come up against unexpected circumstances, they give up or turn back.

The bigger your goals are, the more willing you will be to pay the price. If you are going to set goals then you may as well set goals that will truly be worth all the effort you put in whilst achieving them.

Achieving what you want may involve making lots of changes and sacrifices. You may have to work longer hours, change who you spend your time with, change your habits, wake up earlier, etc. But if it means getting a promotion, earning enough money to enjoy a better lifestyle or looking and feeling great in a new outfit then surely it is worth the sacrifices you will have to make.

The only person who can make that decision is you.

> *"Shoot for the moon. Even if you miss you'll land among the stars"*
>
> **Brian Littrell**

Most people don't aim BIG because they are scared of not reaching their chosen destination. Well I agree with the quote above when it comes to setting goals—I would rather narrowly miss out on a big target than reach a small one. If you aim big, you are much more likely to achieve big. Do not let your fear of failure stop you from shooting for the moon.

Make your goals big enough to stretch you but not so big that they overwhelm you. You want to have goals that in the process of achieving them, you become a better person.

> *"Who will you have to become to achieve all you want?"*
>
> **Anthony Robbins**

Access all areas

Truly successful people understand the importance of setting goals in all areas of their lives. They work hard and play hard. They are not satisfied with success in just one or two areas of their life, they have high standards for their life as a whole and that means everything they do.

> *"When you play, play hard; when you work, don't play at all"*
>
> **Theodore Roosevelt**
>
> —Former US President—

Great achievers understand that how you do anything is how you do everything. Having high standards is an attitude that spills into every area of your life.

Success has a knock-on effect. When you are successful in one area of your life, it rubs off in other areas of your life. That is the nature of balance.

For example; there is no point in working hard in your career to earn lots of money if you neglect your health and cannot enjoy the fruits of your labour. On the flip side, when you focus on both they boost each other. The fitter and healthier you are, the more energy you have to put into your work goals. It is the same with every other area of your life—the happier you are with each area, the more positive emotional energy you will have to pursue other goals. But when you struggle in one area, it robs you of vital energy needed to pursue other areas.

As I said, how you do anything is how you do everything.

Synchronize effort with outcome

When setting your goals, there needs to be a correlation between the size of your goals and how much action you are willing to take and how much you are willing to stretch yourself.

I believe this is the most important distinction in successful goal setting and one which most goal setting methods do not teach.

You can set your goals as BIG as you like, but only in accordance with the amount of effort you are willing to put in. If you are only willing to stretch yourself a little bit, then you need to factor this into your goal setting and how big you aim. If you are willing to completely overhaul your life and make incredible sacrifices then there are no limits to what you can achieve.

Common goal setting techniques focus a lot of attention on the end outcome but the most important goals for you to focus on are the 'performance goals'. These are the day to day actions you are willing to take to achieve your end outcomes.

Examples of performance goals might be; making 20 calls per day, getting up 2 hours earlier each day to hit the gym, practising for an extra hour every day, etc.

You have to decide what price you are willing to pay and a price that you believe will be enough to achieve your desired outcome. For example; in order to find 10 new clients you may need to make an extra 100 calls or setup 50 meetings. Therefore 100 calls or 50 meetings becomes your performance goal.

David Beckham decided early on in his career the price he was willing to pay to become one of the best free kick specialists of all time. He would stay behind after training every day practising free kicks when all the other players had gone home. His manager Sir Alex Ferguson said that "he practised with a discipline to achieve an accuracy that other players wouldn't care about". For David Beckham, spending an extra couple of hours training each day was worth becoming one of the best dead ball strikers of a football the world has ever seen.

What lengths are you willing to go to, to achieve your goals?

I remember having a conversation with the directors of a business who were facing some difficulty in finding new clients and were facing the risk of going under. I asked them how important it was for them to be successful and then asked them what they were willing to do to make sure they found the clients they needed. Once I got them to understand how much it meant to them, they decided on some major action they were willing to take each day. I spoke to them a week later and they had secured more clients in that week than they had in the previous 2 years!

With the right amount of effort, anything is possible.

When I was studying for my diploma in Neuro Linguistic Programming (NLP), which is the study of human excellence, I learnt that there are four clear steps to any outcome you are trying to achieve. These steps are;

1. Decide what you want to achieve

2. Take action

3. Be aware enough to know if you are moving closer or further away from your outcome

4. Be flexible so you can vary your behaviour until you reach your outcome

If you follow these four steps and persist then eventually you can accomplish anything you want.

All great achievers understand the importance of focusing on the practise, the performance goals, the journey rather than the destination. Like I said in the last chapter, top performers focus on giving their best in each moment and the results often take care of themselves.

> *"I know some people say 'Keep your eyes on the prize,' but I disagree. When your eyes are stuck on the prize, you're going to keep stumbling and crashing into things. If you really want to get ahead, you've got to keep your eyes focused on the path."*
>
> **Russell Simmons**
>
> —Music Producer and Entrepreneur—

Have you ever noticed that when you really want something so badly that you totally depend on and rely on it, it very rarely happens? But for some reason, when you are not that bothered, not desperate and approach it with a relaxed attitude that it seems to come much easier?

There is something about desperation that just seems to kill off the attraction of your desires!

Successful people are clear on what they want but they stay focused on the path, giving their full attention to each step along the way, taking it one game at a time until they reach their destination. They let go of the outcome and trust that by giving their full effort to the task at hand, that the final result will take care of itself. This way, they can be satisfied that no matter what the result is, they knew they had given their all.

Success Mapping

How do you eat an elephant?

One bite at a time!

When you have big goals it is easy to feel overwhelmed by the size of them. That is why it is important to break them down into manageable chunks, so you can see just how you are going to achieve them.

By breaking your goals down into clear, specific step by step actions you increase your chances of success dramatically.

> "Nothing is particularly hard if you divide it into small jobs"
>
> **Henry Ford**
>
> —Founder of Ford Motor Company —

Brian Tracy, one of the World's leading authorities on peak performance states that for every minute you spend planning will save you as many as ten in execution. Think about the building of a house. The builders don't just turn up each day with the idea of laying down the bricks on top of each other and hoping it will all come together. They follow a detailed plan from the architect, which means that they are much more likely to avoid mistakes and time wasting activity.

There is an old adage in the British Army known as the 7 P's;

Prior **P**lanning and **P**reparation **P**revents **P**iss **P**oor **P**erformance

They use this adage when it comes to project planning and training for life and death situations. When this adage is explained, the humour and the shock of the mild expletive help to drill home the message and make it memorable!

I like to think of planning of making decisions in advance and this allows me to be much more effective in the present. It allows me to focus on the task at hand instead of thinking of everything else I need to do that day. I am much more likely to apply myself more when I have already decided what I am going to do in advance.

When you have planned in advance, it is much easier to focus in the present. When you fail to plan in advance, it prevents you from giving your all in each present moment because your mind will constantly be trying to work out what to do next. But when you plan effectively in advance, you can give your full attention to the present moment which increases your chances of success dramatically.

I like to use the example of going to the gym. When I go to the gym with my workout planned out, I am much more likely to follow through on that plan and work harder. But when I go to the gym without a plan I am much more likely to slack, take it easy and hit the sauna early! The only person who I am cheating is myself.

Studies show that when you decide in advance what you are going to do, you are much more likely to follow through on your plans.

In one of the most dramatic studies done on this, a group of drug addicts were studied during the withdrawal phase, which is a time when the energy required to control the urge to take drugs severely compromises their ability to perform anything else. The study focused on helping them to find employment after they had undergone rehabilitation. As part of the study, one group was asked to commit to writing a short CV before 5pm on a particular day. Not one person in the group succeeded. A second group was then asked to complete the same task, but they had to say exactly when and where they would write the CV. The results showed that 80% of that group succeeded.

Putting a time and date on exactly when you are going to do something dramatically increases the likelihood you will follow through.

Have you put a date on your goals yet?

Quantum Leaping

How much progress you make and how quickly you make it is totally up to you. You have the potential to catapult your success if you are willing to take a leap, instead of the standard hops taken by the majority.

"Say no to the drug of gradualness. It was Martin Luther King, Jr., who spoke out strongly against making slow changes. Either we risk or we don't, he said. Either we change or we don't. There's no acceptable middle ground because it lulls us into complacency. Lasting changes rarely occur

when we ease our way into the future. They come when we leap. The leap themselves can be small or large. Once we take action, we see things differently and for many of us there's no going back."

Robert K Cooper

-Leadership Expert and Best Selling Author-

What is your quantum leap?

When setting your goals, choose a goal that will represent a quantum leap for you. Whatever that quantum leap is, is totally up to you. Whether it is a promotion at work, starting your own business, running a marathon, winning a gold medal, overcoming a fear of public speaking or finding a life partner!

Whatever that quantum leap is for you in your life, go for it with all your energy and focus and reap the knock-on benefits. My leap was overcoming my fear of public speaking. I gained so much momentum and confidence from making that leap that it had a knock on effect in many areas of my life. That is the magic of taking a leap in your life.

When you take a leap in life, you gain a psychological boost that not only propels you towards your goals and dreams but also builds an inner belief and confidence that lasts forever.

Decide what would quantum leap your life and start the process as soon as possible.

Climb 'Til Your Dream Comes True

Often your tasks will be many and more than you think you can do.

Often the road will be rugged and the hills insurmountable, too.

But always remember, the hills ahead are never as steep as they seem,

And with faith in your heart, start upward and climb 'til you reach your dream.

For nothing in life that is worthy, is ever too hard to achieve,

If you have the courage to try it and you have the faith to believe.

For faith is a force that is greater than knowledge or power or skill,

And many defeats turn to triumph if you trust in gods wisdom and will.

For faith is a mover of mountains, there's nothing that god cannot do,

So start out today with faith in your heart and climb 'til your dream comes true!

Helen Steiner Rice

"Go to Chapter 6 and complete the exercises on creating an exciting vision for your life"

Chapter 3

Limitation Disengage

The two major obstacles to success and achievement are fear and doubt"

Brian Tracy

There is nothing that limits us and holds us back more in our lives than that of fear and doubt. Overcoming fear and doubt are paramount to your success.

It is one thing knowing that we have such infinite potential within ourselves, but how do we maximise this potential?

How can we bridge the gap between what we are capable of and the results we actually produce?

Myles Downey explained this neatly in his book *Effective Coaching* and proposed this formula:

$$Potential - Interference = Performance$$

Timothy Gallwey originally introduced the concept of 'interference' in his groundbreaking book *The Inner Game of Tennis* in 1974.

Interference usually comes in the form of fear and doubt and can usually be found in the following examples;

Fear of failure, fear of success or fear of making a fool of yourself

Lack of self-confidence

Trying too hard

Trying for perfection

Trying to impress

Anger and Frustration

Boredom

A busy mind

How many times do you think one of these things has stopped you performing at your best in any particular task?

I know many of them have got in my way before and it seems that when you experience these, that your mind cannot focus correctly on what you are doing and therefore you don't perform to the best of your capability or potential.

This could be during any task from taking part in a game with friends, to impressing in a work situation such as a presentation or an interview.

It reminds me of a time when I was young and learning a new skill, such as riding a bike. When left to it on my own, just solely focused on the task of riding the bike, I would ride it perfectly. Then my mum or dad would come out to see how I was doing and as soon as I knew they were watching, I would fall off! Can you remember anything like this ever happening to you?

Martin Robert Hall

How often do you think this interference gets in your way each day?

How often does it creep in when you are trying something new?

I remember starting a job after University selling over the phone. Once we had been trained and given the pitch, our calls were monitored to see how we performed. When I wasn't being monitored, I was relaxed and was more successful in dealing with customers. However, as soon as I knew I was being monitored, I was more conscious of my performance and all sorts of interference crept in. Suddenly I was making the most amateur mistakes like getting customer's names wrong, pronouncing words wrong and even on occasion—swearing! Oh dear!!

Most of this interference is ultimately based on fear. Most of the time we are scared of what the resulting outcome will be, whether that is failure, embarrassment, rejection or some other uncomfortable feeling.

Fear comes as a result of imagining a negative outcome. The trouble with this is that the more we imagine this negative outcome happening, the more likely we are to achieve a negative outcome. The more likely we are to mess up, to perform badly, make mistakes or not even try in the first place. Ironically this leads to us achieving the same outcome we were afraid of in the first place.

So why do we have fear if it holds us back from achieving what we want so much?

When I was studying NLP I learnt that we are born with just two fears. 'Just two fears I thought?? Are you kidding'?! Many studies and research show they were not. These two fears are:

Fear of falling.

Fear of loud noises.

We are born with a fear mechanism built within us. This fear mechanism within our bodies was designed to protect us from danger thousands of years ago when we were exposed to dangerous environments, where creatures such as sabre tooth tigers were roaming! This reflex is known as 'fight or flight' and it produces adrenaline within our bodies that provides us with the energy to take action.

Thousands of years ago this adrenaline was very useful in helping us run away from danger but these dangers are much less likely for most of us nowadays. The trouble is that we still have this fear mechanism built within us and as we are growing up, we associate this fear mechanism with many things.

An important thing to note is that all your fears are learned—you were not born with them.

We don't come into this world filled with fear and doubt, can you ever remember seeing a negative baby?!

We learn all of our limits as we are growing up. We learn by modelling everything around us, especially the people in our lives such as parents, teachers and friends. When we get told things like;

"Stop thinking that way, it's just not possible"

"Be sensible and get in the real world"

"No you can't do that or have that"

"You can never do that, stop dreaming"

"You're not good enough"

We end up believing them even if what we are told isn't true. Unfortunately we run the risk of limiting ourselves for the remainder of our lives unless we challenge many of our beliefs and conditioning.

The most extreme case of modelling their environment I have heard of is the story of 'Chicken Boy'. It is the story of a boy who grew up in Fiji and spent his childhood around chickens when his parents died. Local people fed him but nobody took him in so he spent most of his time with the chickens in the village. He adopted all the same behaviours as a chicken and grew up behaving just like a chicken. He didn't stand, he crouched. He didn't speak, he clucked. He moved like a chicken, ate like a chicken and behaved just like a chicken. He didn't even know how to speak or interact with humans.

In 2002 he was discovered by a lady called Elizabeth Clayton on a trip to Fiji. She couldn't believe her eyes when the locals asked her 'have you seen Chicken Boy'??. When she found him, he was 30 years old. For 30 years he had been living his life as a chicken because that is all he knew and learned from being a child. I did say it was an extreme case!

Fortunately, Elizabeth eventually took him home with her and started teaching him new behaviours and how to interact as a human and he has made fabulous progress after a lot of hard work and re-conditioning.

Extreme?

Yes, but it just goes to show how open we are to learning and how easily we are conditioned. As you get older this openness to learning becomes much more restricted and many of us hold on to limiting behaviours and beliefs that we learned when we were not even old enough to understand them.

Making friends with fear

Unfortunately, the feeling of fear is uncomfortable. It often makes us produce feelings we don't like such as sweaty palms, the jitters, butterflies in our stomach, stuttering speech and shortness of breath. In extreme cases it can lead to panic attacks and passing out.

Many people do their utmost to avoid feeling fear because of these uncomfortable feelings. But the danger here is that you run the risk of never really achieving what you want in life because you avoid doing what is necessary. Successful people on the other hand face their fears, they don't let the feeling of fear stop them from doing what they want to do. They act anyway despite the feeling of fear.

We have been conditioned to associate negative feelings with fear and as a result we tend to avoid all the things in our lives with which we associate the feeling of fear.

> *"We should all start to live before we get too old. Fear is stupid. So are regrets"*
>
> **Marilyn Monroe**

One of the ironic things about fear is that most of things we fear never actually happen anyway. We worry about the most ridiculous things at times and they can actually be detrimental to our health. In the book *How to Stop Worrying and Start Living* Dale Carnegie says that 70% of all patients who come to physicians could cure themselves if they got rid of their fears and worries. There are numerous studies that have shown many people who have successfully overcome illness with the power of their mind and many who have worsened their illness and even rapidly accelerated death due to worry.

Stop and think about where your worrying gets you, most of the time it doesn't get you anywhere except to put you in a poor state of mind.

I also learnt whilst studying for my NLP Diploma that the mechanism in our bodies that is responsible for producing fear, is the very same mechanism that produces excitement. However there is one small distinction in the process. And it is this—lack of breath. That is the only difference in the process of your body producing the feeling of fear or producing the feeling of excitement. Small difference wouldn't you agree?

When I first started public speaking I was really nervous and as a result I would speak really fast, hardly take in any breath and end up stuttering and worry even more that people would notice how nervous I was! It was a downward spiral. Once I had done it a few times, I learned to slow down, breathe more, pause in between sentences and as a result I started to enjoy my speeches.

Do I still get the same feelings today that I did when I first started speaking? Yes I do. But now I just acknowledge the feeling, breathe as normal and interpret the feeling as excitement rather than fear. I use it to fuel my performance with passion and energy.

> *"I know that fear is an obstacle for some people but for me it is just an illusion"*
>
> **Michael Jordan**

So what is the best way of dealing with fear?

The best way of dealing with fear is to acknowledge the fear, take big deep breaths and then take action anyway. Always take action or the fear only gets worse. Flip your thinking and see the feelings as excitement and not fear, see it as a positive rather than something negative. Allow yourself to feel the fear, it isn't going to kill you. Yes it may be a bit uncomfortable but it will only stop you if you allow it to.

Start changing the negative associations you have with fear by acknowledging the feeling instead of avoiding it. When you experience the feeling you label as fear, start to see it as excitement instead. The more you do this, the more comfortable you will become with the feeling of fear and eventually there will be no task you fear.

The feeling of fear is not going to go away. It is a mechanism within your body and it's not like a kidney that you can have removed! So you have two choices, you learn to handle it or you avoid it every time it pops up and go through your life avoiding everything that makes you uncomfortable.

Your Operating Zone

We all have an inbuilt psychological thermostat which regulates our actions and behaviours very similar to how a thermostat regulates the heating in your home. When the temperature of the room rises above the setting on the thermostat, the heating will automatically switch off to bring the temperature back within the desired range.

Our inner thermostat works much the same way. It is referred to as the 'comfort zone' and when we operate outside it, our bodies use uncomfortable feelings to keep us within this safety zone.

Our comfort zone is formed throughout our lives by the reinforcement of all the negative thoughts, doubts and fears we have. The more we challenge and step outside our comfort zone, the bigger it gets and the more our confidence grows meaning we find it easier to take on new challenges. However if we always remain within our comfort zone then we run the risk of living safe and never achieving what we are truly capable of.

Most worthwhile and rewarding goals will always be slightly outside your comfort zone. Some call this your 'stretch zone'. If they were not outside your comfort zone then you would not be challenged by them, therefore they would not be satisfying and fulfilling. They would be too easy, boring and would not motivate you to push yourself.

Start seeing your comfort zone being activated as a good thing. Every time you feel your comfort zone being stretched, get excited because this is a signal that you are stretching yourself, applying yourself fully and working towards worthwhile goals.

The more you operate outside your comfort zone, the faster you will achieve everything you want.

Three enemies to success

There are three fears that hold people back from achieving what they want in their lives more than anything else;

The fear of failure

This has to be the biggest and ugliest fear of them all. Successful people learn to deal with failure while unsuccessful people do their best to avoid it at all costs, often meaning they give up before they even begin.

> "I've missed more than 9,000 shots in my career. I've lost almost 300 games. 26 times I have been trusted to take the winning shot and missed. I've failed over and over again in my life and that is why I succeed"
>
> **Michael Jordan**

Great achievers realise that it is impossible not to fail at some point. In fact they realise that failure is just another word for feedback. They know that they never really get any better until they experience failure and they learn from the experience. Successful people see failure as a measure of their progress. They go after it. If they are not experiencing some failure then they are not trying hard enough!

> "There are no failures—just experiences and your reactions to them"
>
> **Tom Krause**

Thomas Watson, the founder of the computer giant IBM once said that 'the fastest way to succeed was to double your failure rate'. I disagree with this slightly, I think that you can go one better and triple or even quadruple your failure rate if you really want! The point is that the more you experience failure, the more likely you are to experience success.

Sir Richard Branson, one of the most successful entrepreneurs in the world, believes that failure is a very important part of succeeding. He said that 'one of the reasons why Virgins enterprises have been so successful over the years is that we have empowered the staff to make mistakes—and then learn from them'. He understands that it is how you respond to failure that matters and key to your success.

Whenever I work with sales people, I tell them that the quickest way to earn more money and get more sales is to change how they feel about failure. The most successful sales people are not bothered by failing, they just brush it off and move on to the next potential customer. Why would they take it personally?

Start to flip your thinking around failure and start seeing it as a natural part of the pathway to success. Expect more of it and celebrate it when it happens because that means you are making progress. Don't take it personally, it is not about you. Just focus on doing your best in each moment, always trying to improve on your last effort.

> "If you're doing your best you won't have any time to worry about failure"
>
> **H Jackson Brown Jr**

The next fear successful people learn to deal with is;

The fear of criticism

It is natural for us to seek approval for our actions in life because as we are growing up we constantly seek the approval of our parents and peers, trying our best to impress them. When we fail to impress them and are criticised for our poor efforts, this lowers our self esteem. Unfortunately for many people, avoiding criticism and the opinions of others can continue throughout their whole lives and stop them from doing what they really want to do.

> *"When you make it a strong habit not to take anything personally, you avoid many upsets in life"*
>
> **Don Miguel Ruiz**

Going through your life holding back, avoiding doing the things you really want because of a fear of what others think is quite ridiculous when you think about it. I am not saying that what other people think does not matter at all—I think the feedback and opinion of those people that have your best interests at heart is very important. But to let the opinions of others hold you back from doing what you really want and being who you really want to be doesn't make sense to me. Especially as most of the time we allow the opinions of people who we don't even like or respect bother us more than any other. Ever noticed that?!

> *"I don't know the key to success, but the key to failure is trying to please everybody"*
>
> **Bill Cosby**
>
> —Famous actor, comedian, author and musician—

It is normally the people who criticise and condemn you who you shouldn't take much notice of anyway. If all they do is criticise you then that says much more about them than it does about you. This doesn't mean that you should avoid criticism completely, it just means that you should be selective who you pay attention to.

Remember this:

It is up to you how you interpret the thoughts and opinions of others.

You can either use it to your advantage or you can let it impact you in a negative way. Just remember that if you do allow it to have a negative impact on you, that is your choice. You don't have to take on board everything everybody says to you. Be selective. See yourself as a strict gatekeeper who only allows constructive and useful feedback through the gates and turn away the harmful and destructive feedback.

Successful people know that no matter what you do in life, some people will praise you, some people will criticise you and some people won't notice you at all. They accept that his is just the way it is and do not let it affect them in any way. You cannot please everybody!

All great achievers have faced criticism and ridicule at some point but they do not let it prevent them from following through with their ideas, plans and actions.

Be selective who you pay attention to, do not allow the opinion of others to prevent you from doing what you believe in and remember that no matter what you do—you will not please everybody. So go forth and do it anyway!

> *"I like to be a free spirit. Some don't like that but that's the way I am"*
>
> **Princess Diana**

And now the third and final fear that holds people back massively;

The fear of rejection

This fear is closely linked to both the fear of failure and criticism. Rejection is another fear that when you analyse it, it doesn't make much sense. It comes down to us not liking to hear the word 'NO'. We don't like to hear this word because it normally leads to the feeling of disappointment.

We get our hopes up, imagine what succeeding would feel like and then we face the possibility of somebody 'saying no' to what we want. This leaves us feeling disappointed. Often we take it personally, we think it is about us and blame ourselves. When most of the time it never really is about us, there are many other factors that could be behind it. You might have asked at a bad time, they might not have what you are asking for, they might have misheard you or they might not be able to give you what you want. Might, might, might!

You will never know if you don't ask. Get used to hearing the word 'no' and accept that it is just part of life. The more you can get used to hearing and dealing with being rejected, the more successful you will be.

Just because you get rejected does not mean you should give up. Sometimes it is just life's way of testing your resolve, making sure you want it badly enough. Successful people respond to rejection by trying harder, by being persistent and by proving that they were wrong to be rejected.

There are many famous people who became successful by ignoring rejection. Sylvester Stallone was famously rejected more than 1500 times in his pursuit of his dream to become an actor. J K Rowling was rejected countless times before she finally got her famous Harry Potter books published, which have now sold well over 300 million copies. The Beatles audition tape was rejected by every single record company in the country and they were famously told that guitar groups were on their way out.

But did they let multiple rejections get in their way of their success?

Did you know that research shows 94% of sales people quit after the fourth call but 60% of all sales are made after the fourth call? This means that 6% of all sales people are getting 60% of the sales while the other 94% compete for 40% of the sales, you do the maths! The key here is to keep on asking, don't take it personally when somebody says no and don't make assumptions either, you're not a mind reader!

Just like failure, rejection does not really exist in the way most people think of it. Think about it, if you ask somebody for something and they say no, it's not like you have lost anything. You never had it in the first place!

You only have something to gain by asking.

If somebody rejects you, you are still in the same place as before you asked, you have not lost a thing. It all depends on how you interpret it.

In fact by not asking, you are rejecting yourself! By not asking you are losing out in advance by not even giving yourself a chance.

What could you ask for?

—A promotion?

—A date?

—The sale?

—Feedback on your performance?

—A negotiation on price?

Whatever it is you need to ask for to move you closer to your goals, just remember that you have nothing to lose. Nothing! Get used to asking more often, you will be amazed at the things you get when you ask. If you are not hearing enough no's then you are not asking enough questions! Flip your fear on rejection and start seeing it as a good thing. The legendary Charlie Chaplin had an interesting view on rejection;

> *"Actors search for rejection. If they don't get it they reject themselves".*

Start seeking out rejection. The more you hear it, the more success you will have.

Success filters

Your experience of the world is filtered through your beliefs. Your beliefs are at the root of all your behaviours and are therefore indirectly responsible for how successful you become. You will struggle to find any successful person who lacks belief in themselves.

> *"The outer conditions of a person's life will always be found to reflect their inner beliefs"*
>
> **James Allen**

Reflection

The most famous sportsman of all time and widely known as 'the greatest' Muhammad Ali was somebody who really understood the importance of believing in yourself and still does.

"I have always believed in myself, even as a young child growing up in Louisville, Ky. My parents instilled a sense of pride and confidence in me, and taught me and my brother that we could be the best at anything.

I must have believed them, because I remember being the neighbourhood marble champion and challenging my neighbourhood buddies to see who could jump the tallest hedges or run a foot race the length of the block. Of course I knew when I made the challenge that I would win. I never even thought of losing."

Optimize Yourself

> "In high school, I boasted weekly - if not daily - that one day I was going to be the heavyweight champion of the world. As part of my boxing training, I would run down Fourth Street in downtown Louisville, darting in and out of local shops, taking just enough time to tell them I was training for the Olympics and I was going to win a gold medal. And when I came back home, I was going to turn pro and become the world heavyweight champion in boxing. I never thought of the possibility of failing - only of the fame and glory I was going to get when I won. I could see it. I could almost feel it. When I proclaimed that I was the "Greatest of All Time," I believed in myself. And I still do.
>
> Throughout my entire boxing career, my belief in my abilities triumphed over the skill of an opponent. My will was stronger than their skills. What I didn't know was that my will would be tested even more when I retired.
>
> In 1984, I was conclusively diagnosed with Parkinson's disease. Since that diagnosis, my symptoms have increased and my ability to speak in audible tones has diminished. If there was anything that would strike at the core of my confidence in myself, it would be this insidious disease. But my confidence and will to continue to live life as I choose won't be compromised.
>
> Early in 1996, I was asked to light the caldron at the Summer Olympic Games in Atlanta. Of course my immediate answer was yes. I never even thought of having Parkinson's or what physical challenges that would present for me."

What you choose to believe is up to you. Believing in yourself is a choice. Your beliefs are defined as what you accept as true in your life and only you can decide on what you believe and what you don't believe.

"I always knew I was destined for greatness"

Oprah Winfrey

Unfortunately due to early childhood programming, many of us have more limiting beliefs about our capabilities than we do empowering beliefs. But as you get older it becomes your responsibility to change your beliefs, to search for reasons why you can achieve what you want and start telling yourself statements such as "I can" and "I will" rather than "I wish I could" and "If only".

Successful people understand that believing in themselves is a choice and crucial if they want to have any chance of success. They understand that their beliefs determine their reality and whatever they believe, they will seek out evidence to prove themselves right. They know that when they believe in themselves, they find more reasons to prove that they do have what it takes to succeed.

"When you believe something is impossible, your mind goes to work for you to prove why. But when you believe, really believe, something can be done, your mind goes to work for you and helps you find the ways to do it."

David J Schwartz

How you interpret events in your life determines your beliefs. If you interpret the events in your life in a positive manner then you develop empowering beliefs but if you interpret life's events as mostly negative then you develop limiting beliefs. It is up to you to change the meaning you place on these events and adopt an optimistic attitude, see the positive side of things and develop empowering beliefs in yourself.

Make your mind work for you and start believing in yourself from now on.

Results Guaranteed

Regardless of any limiting thoughts you may have, there is one thing which is more important and actually it is the real measure of your success. I am talking about your behaviour—it is what you do that counts.

> *"What we believe means nothing unless we reflect that in the way we act"*
>
> **Eckhart Tolle**
>
> —Bestselling author and Spiritual Teacher—

Even though what you fear and believe has a massive impact upon the behaviour you produce, it is the action that determines your results. This action may be the amount of shots you take, the number of calls you make or how many times you ask for what you want but if you don't produce the action, you won't produce the result. It's that simple.

Top performers in every area of life deliver when it matters. They produce the required behaviour that delivers the results. They experience doubt, fear and negative emotions too but they do not let it stop them from doing what they need to do. They act anyway. They learn how to control their emotions.

> *"The day I am not nervous stepping onto the first tee is the day I quit"*
>
> **Tiger Woods**

At the root of most of your behaviour are your emotions. The emotional state you are in at any one time greatly determines the behaviour you produce. If you are in a state of fear and doubt then you are more likely to produce a poor result compared with the results you produce when you are in a confident state.

Research in brain waves shows that the difference between an optimal state (often described as being in 'flow' or 'in the zone') and a stressed state (anxiety and fear) is very small. Your brain waves range from as low as 1-4 Hz when you are in a deep sleep all the way up to 100 Hz when you are highly alert and aroused. What research also shows is that when you are in the state of flow your brain waves are operating at 19 Hz and when you are stressed and anxious your brain is operating at just 21 Hz. So the difference between being in an optimal state of mind and an anxious, stressed state is a mere 2 percent.

See what I mean about a fine line?

The line is so fine in fact that you cannot wait to be in this optimal state of mind before you take action. If you did you would never get anything done. One thing I have learnt about emotions is that no matter how hard you try, you cannot always control them. But the one thing you can always control is your behaviour. You always have control over the action you take and ironically this is also the quickest way to control your emotional state.

There are some brilliant techniques in Chapter four to help you master your emotional state when it matters.

I laugh when I read books that offer every technique under the sun to control your emotional state for nearly every situation you may find yourself in. If you even tried to master your emotions, reduce your fears and be perfectly calm and in an optimal state of mind all of the time then life would be extremely boring! You would also spend all your time preparing to take action instead of actually taking action—and in life the most successful people are the ones who just go and do it, not the ones who are constantly reading, learning, researching and talking about it. Successful people are too busy taking action to be waiting on the sidelines for the perfect time to arrive.

There is a small but crucial difference between talkers and walkers in life and that difference is your behaviour.

Successful people don't wait for the perfect emotion before they take action. They don't wait until they feel motivated or until they are free from fear, they take action regardless and that is why they are successful.

Dan Millman, a former World champion and gymnastics coach says;

"Motivation like all states comes and goes, rises and falls. I certainly didn't feel motivated all the time during my gymnastics career. But I trained 6 days per week for more than 4 hours per day, for years by keeping my eye on the goal. Although motivation comes and goes, you can always rely on your will."

How true. There are so many things that influence your emotional state on a daily basis that trying to control them all the time would drive you insane. Research shows that we have approximately 60,000 thoughts per day. Each of these thoughts has an impact on your emotional state. Can you imagine trying to control this all the time?

When you don't feel like doing something but you take action anyway, this is how you develop and install new behaviours and habits. The more you do it, the more you programme yourself with successful behaviours. Unsuccessful people on the other hand find all sorts of reasons not to follow through because they don't feel like it. This is just your comfort zone in operation and as we have already learnt, your comfort zone is there to be expanded.

"The successful person makes a habit of doing what the failing person doesn't like to do."

Thomas Edison

—Famous for inventing the light bulb—

Ironically the fastest and most reliable way of controlling how you feel is by controlling your behaviour. When you follow through on something when you don't necessarily feel like it, you gain the feelings you were waiting for anyway. You feel amazing and your confidence grows rapidly. But when you keep making excuses and putting things off because you don't feel like it, your confidence is taken away rapidly.

"A good idea if not acted upon produces terrible psychological pain. But a good idea acted upon brings enormous mental satisfaction. Got a good idea? Then do something about it. Use action to cure fear and gain confidence. Here's something to remember: Actions feed and strengthen confidence; inaction in all forms feeds fear. To fight fear, act. To increase fear—wait, put off, postpone."

David Schwartz

Start developing the habit of following through on your plans and actions regardless of how you feel, it is the most common habit that successful people have.

Just like the poem by the legendary Mother Teresa on the next page says "do it anyway".

Anyway

People are often unreasonable, illogical and self centred. Forgive them anyway.

If you are kind, people may accuse you of selfish ulterior motives. Be kind anyway.

If you are successful you will win some false friends and some true enemies. Succeed anyway.

If you are honest and frank, people may cheat you. Be honest and frank anyway.

What you spend years building, someone could destroy overnight. Build anyway.

If you find serenity and happiness, they may be jealous. Be happy anyway.

The good you do today, people will often forget tomorrow. Do good anyway.

Give the world the best you have and it may never be enough. Give the world the best you've got anyway.

You see, in the final analysis, it is between you and god, it was never between you and them anyway.

"Go to Chapter 6 and complete the exercises on developing your winning mindset"

Chapter 4

Optimal Performance
–Application Strategies–

Use only that which works, and take it from any place you can find it"

Bruce Lee

—Famous Martial Artist, Philosopher and Actor—

Successful people are highly effective at doing what they need to do to achieve their goals.

They spend their time wisely, focusing on what is important whilst avoiding what is unnecessary. They are always looking for ways to improve, to keep raising their game and ensuring they perform at the peak of their abilities.

Successful people put to work the principles and methods that help them become more successful and avoid the things that slow them down. In this chapter we will explore these success strategies that will help you achieve what you want faster and easier than ever before.

Pick your own team

"You are the average of the five people you spend the most time with"

Jim Rohn

—Self-made millionaire—

Probably the most important influence on your success is the people you spend your time with. The people you spend time with have an enormous effect on you, they either raise you up or they drag you down. Their thoughts, opinions and attitudes rub off on you. Like the quote says above—you become like the people you spend most of your time with.

Your parents understand the importance of this and that is why they are so protective over the people you hang around with when you are growing up. They know that who you spend time with, you will become like. They know you will adopt the same behaviours as the people you hang around with so they want you to hang around with people that will have a good effect on you.

Sir Alex Ferguson is somebody that understands the importance of having the right people around you and the impact that has on success. He has established a very strong team ethic at Manchester United and has always made it clear that no player is more important than the club. He has instilled a positive winning mentality in all of his players and has never been afraid to remove any player if he feels they are having a negative impact on the team as a whole. He has made lots of difficult decisions in his career for the good of the team. He knows how destructive just one person can be to the team morale and that is why he has never compromised on this principle, no matter who the player is.

> *"Without doubt the most common weakness of all human beings is the habit of leaving their minds open to the negative influence of other people"*

Napoleon Hill

Surrounding yourself with the right people might mean you will have to make some difficult decisions. If you want to be successful you might have to reconsider who you spend your time with.

The British Army has proved itself as one of the most professional and highly regarded military forces in the last 300 years and the reason for this is simple: the quality of the soldiers the army produces.

The army has a strict selection process because it understands the importance of getting the right people. They have certain values and standards each soldier has to meet.

The 6 values the army looks for in each of its solders are;

Selfless commitment
Courage
Discipline
Integrity
Loyalty
Respect for others

They also have standards of behaviour each soldier has to meet, which are;

Obeying the law
Don't offend others
Total Professionalism—being the best.

Successful people also have a strict selection policy when it comes to the people they spend time with. They choose to spend their time with people who have a positive effect on them, who encourage them to be the best they can be and who support them in achieving their goals. They stay away from people who have a negative impact on them and sap their energy.

Are you as selective about who you spend time with?

If you want to be successful, you should be.

> *"If someone sees you flying and they don't think they can fly, they'll tear off your wings or make you feel bad for even trying"*
>
> **Ralph Waldo Emerson**

Start spending time with people who you want to become like and stop spending time with anybody who tries to tear off your wings. Surround yourself with successful people and reduce the amount of time you spend with people who sap your energy.

Professional athletes have a team of coaches and experts who are there to constantly support them in achieving their goals. It is one of the main reasons they remain so focused all year round and are able to maintain gruelling training regimes.

Who do you have to support you in your life?

Who is your support team?

Seek out people who have already achieved what you want and learn from them. Spend time with them, ask them for advice, become friends with them, ask them if you can buy them lunch and pick their brains.

One of the most important reasons for having a team of supportive people around you, and a major reason why athletes and top entrepreneurs and business leaders have teams of coaches and mentors, is because other people hold you accountable for your actions. This means your standards do not slip, at least nowhere near as much, because you have a team of people around you making sure you follow through on what you are capable of and what you said you will do.

I know this has had an enormous impact in my life and I have a team of people to keep me accountable in my business, in my health and in my personal life. This group of people is made up of great friends, personal and business coaches, business mentors and personal trainers. Spending time and regularly checking in with these people and sharing my vision and plans with them helps to keep me focused and driven as I know if I let my standards slip then one of them will be there to pick me up on it. Having that positive support is invaluable and also keeps me on my toes!

Start picking yourself a winning team and your results will take off.

Re-condition yourself

"You are a product of your environment. So choose the environment that will best develop you toward your objectives. Analyse your life in terms of its environment. Are the things around you helping you toward success—or are they holding you back?"

W. Clement Stone

—Self-made millionaire and bestselling author—

Every belief, attitude, behaviour, skill, habit and ounce of knowledge you have today is a result of what you have learned during your lifetime. You have been conditioned into the person you are today and the great thing is, you can re-condition yourself at any point in your life.

Possibly one of the most obvious examples of you being a product of your environment is the way you speak—your accent. We learn how to speak by imitating the people in our environment as we are growing up. Many people have the same accent for most of their life because they spend much of their time in the same area, surrounded by people with similar accents. However, have you ever noticed somebody that has moved to a different part of the country or even another country and after a while their accent starts to change and they start sounding like the people around them?

You are being conditioned all the time. From every conversation you have to everything you read, everything you watch, everything you say and everything you do.

Everything that goes into your mind has an impact on you in one of two ways—positive or negative. It will either help you move towards what you want or it will move you further away from what you want.

> *"The mind is everything. What you think about you become"*
>
> **Buddha**

It is your responsibility to fill your mind with things that will help you succeed and the more you do it, the faster your confidence will grow and the more successful you will become.

According to Martin Seligman, one of the leading psychologists in the World, one of the most significant findings in Psychology in the last twenty years is that individuals can choose the way they think. It is possible to change your thought patterns and therefore direct your thinking in the same way that great achievers think.

The way you have learned to think so far in your life is a direct result of your conditioning and you can start to change that by re-conditioning yourself.

Here are some ways that successful people positively condition themselves;

Reading

There are literally thousands of books from some of the most successful people of all time, sharing their lessons and advice on how they achieved success. Whatever you want to learn about and specialise in, you can pretty much guarantee there will be book about it.

Successful people are avid learners, always looking for ways to improve and learn how they can become even more successful. Like I said at the start of this book, Benjamin Franklin once said you can either buy your wisdom or borrow it. By borrowing it, you save yourself valuable time by learning from the mistakes of others.

Bruce Lee, regarded as one of the most influential figures of the 20th century, attributed much of his success to reading and learning from successful people. He had a personal library of over 2,500 books and would avidly read books on martial arts and personal development. He strongly believed that constant learning and personal growth were the keys to a successful life.

If you were to invest just one hour per day reading books on success, by the end of one year you would have invested over 9 working weeks learning about how to become more successful. That is over 2 months! Imagine the impact that would have on you.

Training Courses

You spend many years of your life at school, learning many valuable skills that set you up for life. You may also argue that there are lots of things you learn about that are no use at all. Either way, you don't have much of a choice what you learn about at school as most of it is part of the curriculum which is decided for you.

You do however have a choice about what you learn about after school and in your own time. There are thousands of training courses that teach the skills and knowledge you need for pretty much anything you want to learn about.

Training courses are a very powerful way of conditioning yourself for success as you surround yourself with like minded people, share insights with each other and learn and process lots of valuable information from the trainers. Essentially you are combining many of the techniques of successful learning (being around the right people, reading, writing, reflecting) and the collective impact of these has a long-lasting positive effect on you.

Jack Canfield, a bestselling author, multi-millionaire and leading success coach, says that if he were to attribute his success to just one thing it would be to the numerous personal development seminars he has attended during his life. He says that we all need outside influences to help us break through our habitual patterns and assist us in creating new ways of thinking and behaving.

I for one could not agree more. I always feel an enormous boost in my confidence, productivity and motivation when I attend any form of personal development training.

Each time I book on a training course I like to see it as 'outsourcing my success'. There are many things that we know if we did them, would make us more successful. So each time I book onto a course which I know I will benefit from, I see it as outsourcing my success because I know I will follow through with it because I have committed to it in advance, especially if I have paid for it!

Start outsourcing your success too.

Reduce idle TV time

One of the most powerful sources of conditioning we expose ourselves to nowadays is television. Research shows that the average person watches over 4 hours of TV per day. That means that by the time you have reached 70 years old you will have spent nearly 12 years of your life sat in front of the TV!

The most alarming factor is that much of what is on TV is nonsense and certainly won't help you to achieve your goals in life. Research from the United States shows that the average child will watch 8,000 murders on TV by the time they finish school and will have seen over 200,000 acts of violence by the time they are eighteen, including 40,000 murders.

Not exactly positive viewing!

Be more selective about what you watch on television, there are many inspirational programmes, documentaries and films that you could watch.

Audio Programmes

Along with books and training courses, another great way to learn the wisdom of others is to listen to audio books and programmes.

There are many different sources of audio including audio books, interviews, podcasts and full training courses. The great thing about audio programmes is that you can combine them with other activities, meaning you don't need any extra time to boost your learning.

You can listen to them whilst driving, whilst commuting to work, whilst exercising or whilst relaxing on the beach when you're on holiday!

Start putting all of these methods into practise and boost your learning, take control of your own conditioning and fast track your success by learning from some of the World's greatest achievers.

Optimize your inner genius

"Don't worry about what the World needs. Ask yourself what makes you come alive and do that. Because what the world needs is people who have come alive"

Dr Howard Thurman

—Author, philosopher and civil rights leader—

We all have things that we are naturally good at, things we do easily and effortlessly. We all develop certain strengths as we are growing up and it is important to identify these strengths and use them to our advantage in as many ways as possible.

The more you organise your life around using your natural strengths, the more successful you will become.

When you spend your time utilising your strengths, you achieve your best results. You produce your best work easily, effortlessly and blissfully—you enjoy what you're doing because it comes to you naturally, without thinking.

One of the most common mistakes that people make is to focus heavily on eliminating weaknesses by identifying them and trying to improve them. Focusing on your weaknesses only reduces your ability to excel and do great things with your natural talents. If only people would spend this time focusing on harnessing their natural strengths, they would enjoy more success, fulfilment and satisfaction in their lives.

The most successful people in business spend their time doing what they do best and they delegate as many of the other tasks as they can to their staff and other people. The most successful sports teams are made up of players who are played to their strengths.

Whilst on an Ancient Wisdom Leadership workshop I learnt that research shows that only 21% of staff are said to feel engaged in their jobs and this is due to the conflict with their personal values and strengths. Staff who don't feel engaged reported that they didn't care about their jobs and as a result they are a lot less productive, motivated and valuable to the company.

If you focus on your natural strengths you will be more productive, engaged and have more purpose in everything that you do.

> "If you can find a way to use your signature strengths at work often, and also see your work as contributing to the greater good, you have a calling. Any job can become a calling, and any calling can become a job. "A physician who views their work as a Job and is simply interested in making a good income does not have a calling, while a garbage collector who sees their work as making the world a cleaner, healthier place could have a calling."

Martin Seligman

—World leading psychologist and bestselling author—

When you organise your life around utilising your natural strengths in as many activities as possible, states like motivation, enjoyment, fulfilment, satisfaction and pleasure come naturally and you don't need to manipulate yourself using fancy techniques into motivating yourself (or dragging yourself along, feet scraping the floor) into following through on what you need to do.

There is a universal notion that success takes hard work and most people interpret hard work as painful. The most successful people do not associate hard work with pain, they associate it with feelings of satisfaction, fulfilment and pleasure and that is because they are doing what they love to do and what comes naturally. Who doesn't want that?

Identifying your natural strengths and talents and then organising the achievement of your goals by focusing on using these strengths as often as you can is possibly one of the most valuable exercises you could ever do.

Some people are fortunate enough to become aware of their natural strengths from an early age while many people can go through their whole lives not knowing their natural strengths because they have never taken the time to discover them.

There are some exercises in Chapter 6 that will help you to identify your natural strengths and utilise them to help you achieve your goals both faster and easier.

Fuel your performance

Time management is a hugely popular concept these days and one of the most common challenges most people face in the pursuit of their goals. Everywhere I go I hear people constantly say that they just don't have enough time to do the things they need to do.

Time isn't the problem. We cannot manage time, we can only manage ourselves.

The idea behind time management techniques is that we organise our day in a structure that allows us to be the most productive, therefore achieving our desired results faster. But the major challenge with this is that our productivity cannot be measured by the amount of time we have but only by the amount of focused attention we can give to a period of time.

> *"The ultimate measure of our lives is not how much time we spend on the planet, but rather how much energy we invest in the time that we have"*
>
> **Jim Loehr**
>
> —Performance psychologist and bestselling author—

I believe one of the major problems we face is that we tend to overestimate how productive we can be in the time we have. We underestimate the difficulty in giving our full attention to any one task and as a result it takes us much longer to complete things. This leaves us disappointed at the end of each day when we have not completed what we intended.

How many times have you listed a number of things to get done on a certain day or over a week, to then be troubled with various 'interference' that I discussed in the last chapter, and not complete what you had intended?

This leads to frustration and stress which lowers our energy levels and further inhibits our levels of productivity. If we are not careful, this pattern can stretch to longer periods of time and manifests itself in what we refer to as 'dry spells', 'ruts' or 'plateaus' that can last for weeks or even months at a time.

We can also develop habits such as working late and being late due to our inability to focus our attention effectively to get things done.

On top of overcoming 'interference', the key to maximal performance is to organise our time in bursts of activity where we can apply maximum concentration to a task meaning we are more effective and productive.

This principle applies whether you are trying to finish a project for work or whether you are a world class athlete needing to focus your full attention in training—focused concentration is the key to maximal performance in any given task.

A classic example here from the world of sport is something I see evidence of every week when I listen to football managers talking about their team's performance. Each week there are lots of players who have made a mistake, which ended up costing them the game and the mistake was due to a lack of concentration. There are many players who have great ability but they cannot seem to concentrate for the whole of the game and they get caught out. It does not matter how much ability they have if they cannot remain fully focused on the game for the whole duration. It is the same with any task in your life, whether it is sport or it is a presentation or an interview at work—when you lose concentration you make vital errors.

Focused attention depends on your ability to concentrate all of your energy to whatever you are doing in the moment—and forget everything else in that moment too. Typically when we refer to 'energy' we mostly think of it as something physical, but the amount of energy we have is much more than just physical.

In the excellent book—The Power of Full Engagement, Jim Loehr and Tony Schwartz explain that maximal performance is fundamentally down to energy management and not time management. By energy, they are referring to the amount of energy you can apply to something at any one time. They describe energy as the 'fundamental currency of high performance' and absolutely key to how productive we are with our time.

There are two key distinctions I would like to focus on for maximising your performance. The first one is the different types of energy. As I said, energy is much more than just something physical—there are four separate but related sources of energy that we must refuel to ensure we can apply ourselves fully in our activities. These are;

Physical; Mental; Emotional; Spiritual

Let's consider these separately;

Physical Energy

The most obvious energy source and also the foundation of all your sources of energy, your physical energy is the most important for sustained performance and sustained performance is the goal, especially if you want to keep making progress in your life. Personally I think looking after your body should be a priority for everybody. Unfortunately many of us are conditioned into treating our bodies badly as we are growing up and not looking after ourselves properly but remember the principle of response-ability. It is up to you to change that. One thing I have definitely noticed is that I cannot remember the last time I met a really fit and healthy person who is unhappy—have you ever noticed that?

They just seem to have more vitality, glow and a zest for life, which when it comes to pursuing your goals effectively, is massively important.

There are three major elements of physical energy—food, exercise and sleep. Each one impacts the level of energy you have and ultimately the amount of focused attention you can sustain in any activity you engage in. It doesn't matter whether you are a professional athlete or you work in an office, whatever your daily activities are—they require energy and the amount of physical energy you have available is down to these three elements.

The more physical energy you have, the more focused attention you can give to each task—ultimately determining the level of your performance.

Your diet is like the fuel you put in a car. Would you put diesel in a petrol engine? Would you water your plants with coffee? I'm hoping you answer these questions with a resounding no! So if you wouldn't treat your car or your plants like that, then don't treat your body like that!

I am not saying you can never indulge in any 'guilty' foods, just not all the time. Apply the 80 percent rule to your diet—eat healthy 80 percent of the time and enjoy whatever you like 20 percent of the time.

What does that mean?

That means that 80 percent of the time you eat whole foods, fresh fruit and vegetables and drink lots of water. You limit the amount of processed foods in your diet. You limit the amount of caffeine you have. I think it is pretty fair to say that we all have a good idea of what is good for our bodies and what is not. Enough said!

Then 20 percent of the time you enjoy whatever foods you fancy. Personally, I have one day per week (Sunday) where I enjoy whatever foods I like and for the rest of the week I eat healthily. This keeps me sane and means that when I do indulge in treats etc, that I enjoy them much more because I don't have them as much.

Exercise is the second part of the equation. You were born with limbs for a reason—to move. The more you move, the better you feel—that is why they are called e-motions!

I don't know about you but I know that each time I start the day with some form of exercise, I have more energy and generally feel better throughout the day compared with the days I don't start with some form of exercise.

The third part of the equation is sleep. Getting adequate rest each night is paramount to energy renewal. Between 6-8 hours is recommended. From what I know about effective sleep, you get the most effective sleep when you have a bedtime routine, i.e. going to bed around the same time each evening and following the same activity before bed—some like to read, some have a snack, some meditate. Choose what works best for you.

Put your physical energy to the top of your priority list and enjoy life to the full. Not only will you feel better about yourself, you will have the vital energy required to pursue a successful vision for your life too. Your level of physical energy is key to the achievement of all your goals.

"So many people spend their health gaining wealth, and then have to spend their wealth to regain their health"

A.J. Materi

Mental Energy

Your mental energy is based upon your ability to focus on one task solely with as little 'interference' as possible. The less 'interference' you have in each moment, the closer you come to being in a 'flow' state or widely known as 'being in the zone'. To understand this state of mind in more depth, please go back to chapter 3.

All great performers have learnt to master their mental energy. They access the optimal state of mind they need when it matters.

I cover specific techniques for improving your mental energy in 'Optimize your mindset' later in this chapter. Your mental energy is also closely related to your physical energy, that is why I covered physical energy first. It is impossible to have great mental energy if you do not have great physical energy—your body and mind directly impact each other.

> *"To keep the body in good health is a duty . . . otherwise we shall not be able to keep our mind strong and clear"*
>
> **Buddha**

Emotional Energy

Are you generally in a positive mood or a negative mood?

The answer that came into your head instantly is the right answer!

Emotional energy is the management of your emotions and your emotions play a massive role in how you behave, which ultimately determines your results.

Successful people understand the importance of keeping their emotional energy high, frequently feeling and displaying states of enthusiasm, confidence, optimism, happiness, fulfilment, gratitude, motivation, satisfaction and any other positive state you can think of.

Positive emotional energy comes as a result of thinking positive thoughts.

You may want to read that again.

"A man is but the product of his thoughts, what he thinks he becomes"

Mahatma Ghandi

—One of the most influential leaders of the 20th Century—

Just like when you provide your body with a nutritious meal—you top up on physical energy, when you flood your mind with positive thoughts—you top up on emotional energy.

If you think positive, uplifting thoughts then you feel positive and uplifted and therefore act in a positive manner. If you think negative thoughts, the opposite occurs.

Jose Mourinho, one of the most successful footballer managers in the world, is someone who believes in keeping his players emotional energy positive.

He calls it the emotional bank account and to keep players positive, you have to make more positive deposits than withdrawals. He classes praise and constructive feedback as a positive deposit and destructive criticism as a withdrawal.

Apply this theory in your life and start making more positive deposits in your emotional bank account. The more you do this, the more positive action you will produce.

Your emotional energy probably has more influence over your ability to take action than all your other energy sources, but the reason it does not come above physical energy is because it is no good feeling great if you don't have the physical energy to carry out what you need to do to achieve your goals.

Saying that, it is very closely linked to your physical energy as the more physical energy you have—naturally the better you feel emotionally.

I will give you some effective techniques for raising your emotional energy later in this chapter.

Spiritual Energy

Spiritual energy may not necessarily be what you think it is. It has nothing to do with religion as a lot of people associate it with.

When you are high in spiritual energy, it simply means a time when you are in 'high spirits'. We all have times when we are high in spirits, feeling inspired and excited by life and this is exactly what your spiritual energy reflects.

When do you feel most inspired by life?

When do you feel most content?

When do you feel most at peace?

These are the times when you are in high spirits, when you feel inspired by life.

Successful people are high in spirits because they have an inspired vision for their life, they know where they are going in their life and what their life is about. Having this inspired vision and clarity fills them with spiritual energy and this energy drives them towards their goals with what can only be described as an invisible force.

They experience this energy because they are pursuing goals that give their life purpose and meaning. Being high in spirits has a knock on effect on all your other energy sources.

Your answers to the three questions above will give you some indication of what inspires you most about your life. Start doing more of these things and your life will feel like it has taken off.

I know when I am incorporating more of these activities in my life, I feel amazing. The best thing about these activities is that they are often very simple. Some of mine are enjoying a cappuccino whilst reading the Sunday paper, socialising with friends and spending time with my favourite animals—dogs. I have a list of about 20 different activities so I always have options to feel inspired!

Deepak Chopra, one of the leading authorities in the World on raising your spiritual energy, has this to say on the topic which I think sums up spiritual energy superbly;

"Success in life could be defined as the continued expansion of happiness and the progressive realization of worthy goals. Success is the ability to fulfil your desires with effortless ease. And yet success, including the creation of wealth, has always been considered to be a process that requires hard work, and it is often considered to be at the expense of others. We need a more spiritual approach to success and affluence, which is the abundant flow of all good things to you. With the knowledge and practice of spiritual law, we put ourselves in harmony with nature and create with carefreeness, joy, and love."

Inject some inspiration into your life by identifying your 'high spirited' activities and working at least one or two of them into every day.

You will immediately feel the difference.

Recharging

The second distinction I want to talk to you about when it comes to maximising your performance is 'energy recovery'. This is simply about recharging your batteries to ensure maximal performance and making sure you avoid burnout and exhaustion.

All of your four energy sources work in a similar way to a rechargeable battery—they never run out completely but they definitely run low and need regular recharging.

Professional athletes ensure optimal recovery with a process called periodization. This is simply a work-rest ratio that allows the body to recover, grow and come back stronger. The same principle applies to managing your energy levels regardless of your activities.

We live in a world where everything is moving at a fast pace and many people think they can maintain long hours, long weeks and long months without adequate rest and recovery. Ironically this approach leads them to being much more stressed, much less productive and overall considerably less successful but because they feel as though they are working hard—they continue with this approach.

It is just a negative pattern that needs to be broken.

If you approach life like this and feel like it never stops, like you're on a hamster wheel, the danger is that you end up 'hitting the wall' just like some athletes do when they reach a stage in their performance when they simply cannot carry on.

This causes the opposite result you were aiming for in the first place and you only stand to lose with this approach.

> *"Sometimes the most urgent thing you can possibly do is take a complete rest"*

Ashleigh Brilliant

—Author and famous cartoonist—

However, if you understand the work-rest principle and apply it effectively in your life, you will experience periods of superior productivity mixed with bouts of highly relaxing and energising rest. By utilising this principle effectively you will be operating your body at the rhythm it was designed to operate at and as a result, your performance will go through the roof.

The key lies in building your day to day activities around specific work-rest ratios.

The key to making consistent and impressive progress towards your long term goals also lies in breaking the goal down into smaller goals in which you apply the work-rest ratio.

Approaching your goals like an athlete engages in interval training is the key to maximal performance and productivity. Interval training is based on the premise that a greater amount of intense work can be accomplished if the work is interspersed with periods of rest and it is much the same with any goal you are trying to achieve.

Breaking your day down into 90 minute intervals interspersed with 10 minute breaks is a much more productive method than just listing everything you need to do each day and working through it with no method. Depending on your ability to apply focused attention you may want to decrease this to 60 minute intervals to start and progress up to 120 minute work intervals.

These intervals fit nicely with the most effective eating patterns for maximal energy return, which is consuming smaller meals every 3-4 hours. This prevents the typical 'energy slump' brought on by eating a big lunch and then trying to perk yourself up by drinking a big cup of coffee!

Start organising your daily tasks in chunks of between 60 and 120 minute blocks, where you give something your undivided attention. Break these chunks up with a short break, which may include going to the toilet, getting a drink or getting some fresh air.

Like anything, it takes practise to master the process and once you do, your levels of concentration will rapidly improve along with your levels of productivity.

In terms of applying the most optimal work-rest ratio to longer periods of time, there are a few options. Each week it is much more productive to take at least one full day off where you totally rest (by this I mean engage only in fun, non-work activities—you know what they are!) than to spread your workload over 7 days.

Try breaking your yearly goals down into monthly projects, with a short break planned at the end of each monthly period. Athlete's fitness programmes are mostly designed around 3-6 week cycles for optimal results because research shows that this is long enough to make significant progress but also not too far away that you lose interest. When you organise your goals on the same premise as this, it is easier to maintain optimal performance.

Tim Ferris, author of the bestseller The Four Hour Work Week, which is entitled that because he reduced his work hours down to such a small portion of time by being ruthless with what he spent his time doing, cutting out time wasting activities and strategically focusing only on the things that delivered the best results, says that everything popular is wrong. He explains that when he was in sales, he started spending one hour making his sales calls between 8 and 8.30am and 6 and 6.30pm each day when he was more likely to get hold of decision makers. By doing this he was able to make twice as many appointments as the people slogging the phones from 9-5! Tim says that being selective and fully focusing for short periods of time does not mean you are lazy, which is what conventional thinking would tell you. He says that most people measure their effort by the total amount of time they put in, instead of measuring it by the effort they put in and results they achieve.

As I said, the typical approach to life nowadays is that we always need to be 'busy' but this is counter-productive. Start breaking the conventional methods and applying yourself fully with bursts of activity and bouts of rest and watch all of your energy sources take off.

Here is a quote which I think perfectly sums up this chapter:

> *"Think for a moment about the look of many long-distance runners: gaunt, sallow, slightly sunken and emotionally flat. Now visualize a sprinter such as Marion Jones or Michael Johnson. Sprinters typically look powerful, bursting with energy and eager to push themselves to their limits. The explanation is simple. No matter how intense the demand they face, the finish line is clearly visible 100 or 200 meters down the track. We, too, must learn to live our own lives as a series of sprints—fully engaging for periods of time, and then fully disengaging and seeking renewal before jumping back into the fray to face whatever challenges confront us."*

Jim Loehr & Tony Schwartz

Apply the work-rest ratio in your life and watch your productivity, effectiveness and energy levels soar to new heights.

Minimal Effort—Maximum Results

Less is more—ever heard that before? Here is why . . .

There is a famous principle which was discovered by a man named Vilfredo Pareto in 1897 which became known as the 'Pareto Principle' and is used by leaders all over the world to help them achieve greater results in less time.

Vilfredo Pareto was an Italian economist and whilst he was studying the distribution of wealth in England, he discovered something very interesting. He found that most of the land in England was owned by a minority of the population. More precisely, he found that 20 percent of the population controlled 80 percent of the wealth and income in the country.

Upon further investigation of this principle, other people also found that this ratio applied to many other things in life. It also applied in other countries all around the world and it was even found to apply to things such as growing your own vegetables! It was found that 80 percent of peas harvested came from 20 percent of the pods.

The 'Pareto Principle' later became popularised as the 80-20 rule and has been written about by many different authors to date.

In one of the most in depth books on the 80-20 rule, Richard Koch gives us many other examples where this rule shows up in our lives;

20% of motorists account for 80% of accidents

20% of married individuals account for 80% of divorces

20% of your carpet probably gets 80% of the wear

20% of your clothes are worn 80% of the time

20% of streets account for 80% of the traffic

20% of clients usually account for 80% of profits

Simply put—you will find that 80 percent of your results stem from 20 percent of your actions.

That also means that 80 percent of what you are spending your time on only leads to 20 percent of your results. Put more bluntly—you are wasting 80 percent of your time on things that aren't important!

By applying this principle in your life, you can generate the results you want in less time, with less effort and less stress. It just means you need to identify your 20 percent activities in the areas of your life you want to improve.

In your financial life, 20 percent of your activity/customers/sales generate 80 percent of your income. Do you know what those 20 percent activities are? Are you doing them often?

In your personal life, 20 percent of the people you spend time with generally contribute to 80 percent of your enjoyment. Who are they? How much time do you spend with them?

You can apply this principle to every area of your life to achieve your best results faster.

"Things which matter most must never be at the mercy of things that matter least."

Johann Wolfgang von Goethe

—Described as one of the most important thinkers of Western culture—

Identifying your top 20 percent activities is an extremely valuable activity you can do but it does not mean it will always be easy focusing on the top 20 percent. If it was, there would be no such ratio because everybody would always do the top 20 percent and there would be no 80 percent left! The reason why everybody isn't applying this principle is because normally your top 20 percent activities are either the most uncomfortable or require your focused attention.

If generating more business or money is what you want it probably means speaking to more people and asking more people for the sale—not sending out a few emails! If it is fine tuning your body you want, it means doing the exercises that require the most effort—not lying in the sauna!

When you identify what these top 20 percent activities are, you will see why most people waste 80 percent of their time—because it is easier to! But that is not why you are reading this book, you are reading it because you want to achieve what you are capable of and reach your goals faster than ever before.

So start by identifying your 20 percent activities in every area of your life and spend 80 percent of your time on them and you can achieve your goals up to four times faster.

As George Bernard Shaw, the famous play writer said;

"The reasonable man adapts himself to the world. The unreasonable one persists in trying to adapt the world to himself. Therefore, all progress depends on the unreasonable man."

Get unreasonable with your time and spend it on the top 20 percent.

Martin Robert Hall

Make a pledge

"We are what we repeatedly do. Excellence, then, is not an act, but a habit."

Aristotle

—Greek Philosopher and one of the most important figures in Western Philosophy—

Psychologist research shows that up to 90 percent of our behaviour is habitual. Most of your behaviours, from the way you walk, talk, drive, think and all the way down to how you brush your teeth is habitual. That means that you don't think about it, you just do it.

Most of your behaviours are learned and then they quickly become habits, often without us even becoming aware of them. Our brains learn to work in this manner so we don't have to learn how to do everything all over again—imagine waking up each morning and having to learn how to brush your teeth?!

The dangerous thing about habits is that if you adopt limiting behaviours and eventually limiting habits without being fully aware of them, you can automatically prevent yourself from achieving success.

On the flip side, it is possible to adopt successful habits and that way automatically succeed.

"The person who wants to reach the top in business must appreciate the might and force of habit. He must be quick to break those habits that can break him and adopt those

practices that will become the habits that help him achieve the success he desires"

J. Paul Getty

—Multi-Billionaire and Founder of Getty Oil Company—

I for one understand the importance of developing positive habits. One of the most positive habits I decided to develop before I started my business was the habit of waking up early. I have since tried to adopt many more positive habits with mixed results. What I have found is that generally, habits are associated generally with being negative. You hear a lot of people often comment about a certain negative behaviour of theirs by saying "it's just a habit I've gotten into".

Generally we refer to our habits as negative and don't question them so much because we do them so often.

Installing new habits takes a lot of awareness and commitment. Because habits are automatic behaviours that we conduct sub-consciously, we need to be really aware and focused on breaking old habits and forming new ones as it is so easy to fall back into old ways.

For this reason, I believe that by making a stronger commitment to a new behaviour in the form of a pledge is much more powerful. By making a pledge, you are making a strong commitment to something and signalling to your brain that it is more than just another habit, which you mostly associate as negative.

Committing yourself fully to something leaves no room for excuses.

"Ninety-nine percent commitment is not possible. We are either 100 percent or not committed at all. I was amazed to discover

this, because I had made a lifestyle out of tepid commitments that turned out to be non-commitments. I was just conning myself that I was partly committed. I had adapted to the pain of early rejection with the decision 'Don't play.' If I didn't play, I wouldn't have to face losing. And if I were forced to play, I could always play half heartedly. If I lost, I could say it didn't matter, because I wasn't trying. It took me many years to realize that I wasn't even in the game if I was not committed. My body might have been out on the field, but my soul was on the bench. Soulless play is worse than no play at all."

Dr Gay Hendricks

—Bestselling author and leading psychologist—

When you make such a commitment it actually becomes easier to follow through on because it is something that you will not negotiate on—you are fully committed to it.

What pledges could you make in your life to guarantee your success?

Getting up early? Setting goals and reviewing them every month? Focusing on your 20 percent activities? Eating a healthy diet? Drinking more water? Visualising your success? Spending time with successful people? Reading for an hour per day? Becoming a non-smoker?

What are the things that if you made a pledge to, would almost guarantee your success?

Consider them carefully and then commit fully to some new behaviour's that will automatically generate you some great results.

Positive Reinforcement

One of the most powerful ways to ensure positive change is to reinforce each change in a positive manner. When we are growing up, we are often rewarded by lots of "well done" comments, hugs, kisses and prizes for achieving something new. Each time we are rewarded for any positive behaviour we are being conditioned to believe that rewards come as a result of producing a positive action.

This conditioning becomes instilled in us and as a result, one of the most powerful motivators of positive change is reward. Rewards come in many forms, ranging from things such as praise, financial rewards and awards and trophies to recognise our achievements.

When you are making changes in your life, the power of rewarding yourself should not be disregarded. We have been conditioned to expect a reward when we have achieved something and you can use this conditioning to your advantage and keep you taking positive action towards your goals.

This is why it is important to have an exciting vision—so the pleasure of achieving it outweighs the pain of getting off your butt and working at it!

Rewarding yourself along the way is an extremely powerful strategy to make sure you follow through and stay on track. When you make pledges to new successful behaviours, build in a regular reward system to keep you motivated.

For example, I reward myself once per week for eating healthy and training hard by enjoying a day where I can eat whatever I like. This keeps me motivated and incentivised to keep taking positive action. I also enjoy the foods much more this way too because I have had to earn them!

How will you reward your successes?

Get creative and reward yourself with something you will really enjoy.

Great companies keep their staff motivated with employee incentive programmes. Professional sports clubs keep their players motivated by rewarding them with regular 'player of the month' awards.

When I started my first business with a friend, we used to set ourselves regular targets and rewards to keep ourselves motivated. As a result we worked harder and enjoyed it much more because we also had something extra to enjoy at the end.

What rewards could you introduce that would really fire up your motivation?

Optimize Your Mindset

I have given many examples so far in this book about how important your mind is. As Buddha said "your mind is everything".

How you use your mind is within your control. Most people don't learn how to run their minds effectively and as a result they struggle to achieve the levels of success they truly desire.

Taking control of your mind is a critical factor when it comes to applying many of the strategies successful people use that I have covered so far in this book. Let's examine some of them further;

Seeing is believing

Seeing the desired result in your mind in advance of it actually happening is something all great achievers do. They can conjure up clear images of them being successful in the future by running inspiring pictures and movies through their mind on a regular basis.

Psychologists call this process mental rehearsal. Research shows that your mind does not know the difference between an imagined experience and an actual experience. Therefore, mental rehearsal is a very powerful method of preparing yourself in advance to make sure that you perform at your very best when it counts.

Athletes understand the importance of mental rehearsal and constantly visualise themselves winning and performing at their best. This prepares them for when crunch time comes, to make sure they are in the best possible state of mind to deliver a winning performance.

There have been many studies conducted that prove the effectiveness of mental rehearsal. One study carried out by Dr Blaslotto at the University of Chicago saw him take a group of basketball players and split them into three groups and tested them on how many free throws they could make. After this initial test, he had the first group practise free throws every day for an hour. The second group just visualised themselves making free throws and the third group didn't do any practise at all. After 30 days he tested them again. The first group had improved by 24 percent. The second group improved by 23 percent and they never even touched a basketball during this period! The third group didn't improve at all.

I remember using mental rehearsal to overcome my fear of public speaking. During one of my first organised events when I had family and friends coming along, I wanted to make sure I delivered a good performance. I imagined everything going perfectly from the guests arriving through to the actual speech and afterwards having people come and tell me how well I did and how much they enjoyed it. On the night, everything went to plan just how I had visualised it in my mind and to this day I can still recall how amazing I felt afterwards!

If that isn't enough to convince you of the power of visualising your perfect future, here is what swimmer Michael Phelps, the most successful Olympian of all time and winner of the most gold medals in a single Olympics, has to say;

"I can visualise how I want the perfect race to go. I can see the start, the strokes, the walls, the turns, the finish, the strategy, all of it. It's so vivid that I can vividly see incredible detail, down even to the wake behind me. It's my imagination at work and I have a big imagination. Visualising like this is like programming a race in my head and that programming sometimes seems to make it happen just as I had imagined it."

So just like Ali, Phelps and all other successful people who can clearly see their ideal future in their minds before it has actually happened, start creating images of your ideal results in your mind and programme yourself for success.

Here are some techniques used by athletes and many other successful people, which I have also used effectively myself and will surely help you to create a clear visual of what you want to see in your future;

Use pictures to trigger the visual process.

There is a technique called fixed visualisation and it involves you looking at a picture of something—it may be of yourself or somebody else, something you want to own or something that reminds you of a certain result you are trying to achieve.

Keep your eyes fixed on the image for at least two minutes and imagine bringing the picture to life, imagine stepping into the picture and being there for real. The more senses you use the better—what do you see?

What can you hear? What can you feel? What can you smell? What can you taste?

The use of images to help trigger the visualisation process is a very common one and used by many successful people who have pictures of their achievements, happy memories and their goals they are working towards where they can see them so they provide a constant reminder of the positive things in their life. The mind thinks in pictures so the more positive images you run through your mind, the more effective it is in helping you perform at your best.

The more you run exciting, positive, uplifting, successful images through your mind, the more optimally your mind will work for you.

Make this a daily practise and see yourself succeeding in your mind first.

Clear your mind

Remember this formula from Chapter three?

$$Potential - Interference = Performance$$

In chapter three, I covered the importance of reducing 'interference' in your mind as it gets in the way of your performance more than anything else, namely in the form of fear and doubt. The less 'interference' you have going on, the more clear your mind is to focus on what you are doing and this is when you produce your best performances. Some call it being in 'flow' or 'in the zone'.

"Empty your mind, be formless, shapeless—like water. Now you put water into a cup, it becomes *the cup, you put water into a bottle, it becomes the bottle, you put it in a teapot, it becomes the teapot. Now water can flow or it can crash. Be water, my friend."*

Bruce Lee

—Famous Martial Artist, Philosopher and Actor—

As Bruce Lee said, empty your mind and it can adapt to whatever you ask of it. Emptying your mind is something we are not too familiar with in the Western world because we are too busy with 'things constantly on our minds'. However, when your mind is constantly buzzing from one thing to the next, it never rests, slows down, recharges and therefore never has time to work optimally for you.

Accessing the state of 'flow' or getting 'in the zone' where you are fully focused, requires a certain state of mind. A state of mind where your mind is not buzzing from one thing to the next and you can train your mind to access this state through the practise of meditation.

Meditation is the art of training your mind to focus and enhancing your ability to bring your full attention and awareness to the present moment.

There are many forms of meditation, from simple breathing meditations to guided meditations that use visualisation methods. Choosing a meditation practise is your choice and what works best for you. There are multiple benefits to meditation and it has been promoted as an incredibly valuable practise for thousands of years.

By meditating, you are training your mind to improve its ability to focus and concentrate which is crucial to your performance as I mentioned before when talking about your mental energy. Meditation is about being in the moment and it is only when you are in the moment, can you be fully focused and effective.

I won't go into all the research and evidence of the benefits of meditation because there is enough to write a book or three! But it isn't just me who understands how valuable meditation is, here are some people who also believe or believed strongly in meditating;

Albert Einstein, Thomas Edison, Leonardo Da Vinci, Jesus, Ghandi, Muhammad Ali, Bruce Lee, Bob Marley, Steve Jobs, Gwyneth Paltrow, Moby, Jennifer Aniston, Richard Gere, Jim Carrey, Jet li, Barack Obama and even famous sports teams such as the Chicago Bulls are using meditation to improve their game.

Make meditation part of your daily practise for endless benefits and turbo charge your performance.

Tell yourself you can do it

The most powerful influence over your emotions and ultimately your behaviour is the way you speak to yourself. Psychologists refer to this as 'self talk' and it plays an enormous role in how you act.

Research shows that we speak to ourselves up to 50,000 times per day. So just in case you were wondering, no you are not going mad for speaking to yourself—we all do it!

If you are communicating with yourself, commenting on everything you are doing, thinking and feeling every minute then you can imagine the effect it has on the results you produce.

Alarmingly, psychologist research shows that most of these conversations we have with ourselves are negative—about 80 percent of them. Have you noticed your patterns of self-talk? Do you regularly encourage yourself with positive comments like "I can do it" or do you slam yourself down with comments like "I can't believe ive messed up again" and "there's just no point, I'll never do it"?

How you speak to yourself has a direct impact on how you perform. It affects your response-ability that we covered in chapter one, it accounts for nearly all of your interference that we covered in chapter three and also has massive impact on your beliefs and behaviours too.

> *"Relentless, repetitive self talk is what changes our self-image".*
>
> **Dr Denis Waitley**
>
> —Bestselling author and consultant on human performance—

The best way to control your self-talk and to build positive self-talk is to construct your own positive statements that you reaffirm to yourself on a regular basis. Positive statements have been used by many of the World's most successful people time and again to build a strong belief in themselves. People use different terms to describe them such as affirmations and mantra's.

One of the most famous affirmations of all time was Muhammad Ali's "I am the Greatest". You can go back to page 49 and read him talking about it again. He used this statement to enhance his belief in himself and other people's belief in him too.

Upon arriving in England in Jose Mourinho, now considered one of the greatest footballer managers in the world, said to the press "Please don't call me arrogant, but I'm European champion and I think I'm a special one". He has since told everyone he is the 'special one' which is his way of building belief in himself and others' belief in him, similar to what Muhammad Ali did. Since that moment, the press have always referred to him as the special one. That one statement has influenced the way millions of people think of him.

Athletes use positive self-talk as part of their mental preparation to ensure they have a fully optimized mindset ahead of their performance. It is not just athletes who use them though, they have been used by many others too;

Leonardo da Vinci, not only a famous artist (mona lisa, last supper) but also an incredible inventor, military engineer, musician, scientist and amazing athlete too, believed very much in the power of affirmations and regularly wrote them down in his journal such as 'obstacles do not bend me' and 'I shall continue'. Even he knew the power of positive self-talk statements all the way back in the 1400's.

Positive self-talk statements are one of the most powerful ways to control your state of mind because it is your internal self-talk that determines most of your feelings and behaviour.

Start coming up with your own affirmations that affirm your greatness and build your belief in yourself and repeat them on a regular basis.

Time for Reflection

Dedicating time for reflection and analysis of your goals, your progress and your life is key to achieving sustained progress and success. You cannot improve without identifying where you need to improve. And you cannot make sure that you keep doing the things that are working if you don't know what those things are.

Taking time out of your 'busy schedule' to relax and have some quality thinking time is similar to the principle of meditation, visualisation and managing your work-rest ratio's in that it goes against conventional approaches that you must keep manically busy!

By taking time out to think and reflect, you ensure you are much more productive and effective and not running round in circles wasting time doing things that don't work.

> *"Saying you're too busy to slow down and give time for yourself is like saying you're too busy to stop for fuel. It doesn't add up!"*

Robin Sharma

— Voted #2 Leadership Guru in the World —

Successful people know that quality results come as a result of quality thinking and quality thinking cannot be done whilst you are driving to work, cleaning the house or in the gym! Quality thinking needs to be a sole task, not a multi-task. It needs to be given your undivided attention and full focus.

The most powerful way of generating quality thinking is to ask yourself quality questions. You cannot come up with the answers you need unless you ask the right questions.

So what are the answers you need to know?

What questions do you need to ask yourself?

We tend to ask ourselves mainly poor questions such as 'why has this gone wrong'? or 'why does this keep happening to me'? instead of questions that will lead us to better answers such as 'what is the lesson to learn here'? and 'how can I turn this around'? and 'how can I make this even better'?

Powerful questions help us tap into what neuroscientists describe as our super-conscious mind. Some of the greatest thinkers and creators of all time, spent hours upon hours in deep thought, questioning themselves until they came up with the answers they needed.

People such as Albert Einstein, Leonardo da Vinci and the Wright Brothers who designed the World's first ever aeroplane. They all understood the power of quality thinking.

"A prudent question is one half of wisdom"

Francis Bacon

—Philosopher, scientist, lawyer and author—

One of the most valuable exercises you can do when you have a problem, are stuck on something or need some clarity on a subject is to write yourself a question at the top of a piece of paper and then write down as many answers as you can, emptying your mind of all its answers. Normally it is the last things that you think of that are the best answers because you have cleared your mind and it works more optimally as it is in a more optimal state. This technique has been said to help you tap into your super-conscious mind, which scientists estimate is up to 10 million times more powerful than your rational thinking conscious mind!

Author Michael Gelb who wrote a book called 'How to think like Leonardo da Vinci' explains a very powerful exercise you can do, based upon an approach by Leonardo da Vinci that was to be curious about life. He calls it One Hundred Questions. The exercise requires you to give yourself 60 minutes where you won't be disturbed and make a list of 100 questions you find interesting. Write about whatever is meaningful for you. Questions can be about anything you like, from 'why does the earth spin'? to 'how can I earn more money' and 'what am I most passionate about'? You may hit some mental blocks doing this exercise, but persist and finish the list in one sitting. Once you have the list, consider the themes of the questions and what most of them are about—whether it is financial, relationships, career, family, personal growth etc. Then refine your list of 100 questions down to your top 10. Then you will have a pretty good idea of what is significant to you in life.

Take time out for regular reflection and quality thinking. Think about your goals, your challenges and your successes. Think about how you could improve, what you could do less of and what you could do more of.

Many people avoid thinking about their situation and how to improve it because it means facing up to things squarely and this can often be uncomfortable. Successful people accept this however and face up to it anyway because they know it is the only way to keep improving.

Clarity does not come by magic. Clarity comes from quality thinking and this requires quality thinking time.

Make it a regular practise of your own.

Start the day with a bang

The most important part of your day is the first hour of it. How you start your day has an overall impact on the rest of your day more than any other time of the day.

Scientific studies show that this is partly because your brain is more susceptible to influence at this time as it comes round from sleep and you are still in a relaxed state of mind. Your brain waves are operating at a lower frequency and this means you can influence your state of mind more powerfully.

> "When you arise in the morning, think of what a precious privilege it is to be alive—to breathe, to think, to enjoy, to love."
>
> **Marcus Aurelius**
>
> —Roman Emperor from 161-180—

There are lots of successful people who swear by their positive routines and starts to the day that include things like;

Getting up early, exercising, reading inspirational stories, meditating and visualising their success, thinking of all the things they are grateful for.

My great grandma was bed bound and she installed the belief in her family that if you can get out of bed in the morning, then you should thank yourself lucky.

How do you start the day?

"When I start my day by reflecting on all the things I have to be grateful for, I'll have a much more rewarding day."

Russell Simmons

—Music Producer and Entrepreneur—

Take charge of your day, give yourself the best possible start and create yourself a routine that guarantees you a positive start to the day and note the difference.

Bringing it all together

So far in this chapter and throughout the book there has been many methods I have shared with you to maximise your performance and achieve all that you want and the key is in bringing it all together to make sure you not only remember it but also practise it.

Some of the principles will work for you, some may not but there are many and remembering them all may prove tricky if you have no way of recording your successful practises.

Martin Robert Hall

I am referring to what I call a 'focus journal'.

This is somewhere where you write down all your goals, you keep images of things you are working towards, you write down your plans and actions, your learning's, your successes, your positive self-talk statements and every other technique that you have found useful so far from this book.

You can keep inspirational quotes in it, inspirational and happy pictures from your life and for what you want to create in the future. It is your own success journal, where you keep everything you want to focus on in your life.

Having a journal is nothing new. Many people have them. Athletes often have them to record their performances and personal best's etc. Successful entrepreneurs use them to capture their best ideas and plans.

Some of the World's most successful people have kept journals. From the likes of Albert Einstein, Leonardo da Vinci and Bruce Lee. In 1994, Bill Gates actually purchased 18 sheets (there is 7,000 of them) from Leonardo da Vinci's journals for $30.8 million!

Dr Kerry Spackman, a Neuroscientist who has worked with many elite athletes has each of them create what he calls a 'winners bible', which contains all of their goals and pictures of the things they want to achieve in their careers to boost their performance, keep them focused and constantly moving towards their ultimate vision.

Some people even create their own creed for how they live their life, the values and the attitudes they want to display each day and then read it each morning.

Here is a creed popularised as 'The Optimists Creed', which was first written by Christian D Carlson and published in 1912. The creed has been used in hospitals to help cure patients and in team changing rooms to help motivate players. I think is a great way to round up this chapter;

Promise Yourself

To be so strong that nothing can disturb your peace of mind.

To talk health, happiness, and prosperity to every person you meet.

To make all your friends feel that there is something worthwhile in them.

To look at the sunny side of everything and make your optimism come true.

To think only of the best, to work only for the best and to expect only the best.

To be just as enthusiastic about the success of others as you are about your own.

To forget the mistakes of the past and press on to the achievements of the future.

To wear a cheerful expression at all times and give a smile to every living creature.

To give so much time to improving yourself that you have no time to criticize others.

To be too large for worry, too noble for anger, too strong for fear, and too happy to permit the presence of trouble.

To think well of yourself and to proclaim this fact to the world, not in loud word, but in great deeds.

To live in the faith that the whole world is on your side, so long as you are true to the best that is in you

"Go to Chapter 6 and complete the exercises on developing your own optimal performance strategies"

Chapter 5

Just Do It

"Knowing is not enough; we must apply. Willing is not enough; we must do"

Bruce Lee

—Famous Martial Artist, Philosopher and Actor—

I started the last chapter with a quote from Bruce Lee and this one also perfectly captures the message in this final chapter. Bruce Lee was somebody who didn't just know, he applied. He applied more than probably any other martial artist in the same amount of time and that is why he became so successful. He was always applying what he learnt because he understood that no matter how much you know, it is no use if you do not apply it.

Hopefully you have learned some great insights and strategies from this book that will help you to become more successful in less time. Now it is up to you to put them into practise and make them work for you. The sooner you do this, the more you will benefit from them and the more likely you will actually follow through.

"Don't put off until tomorrow what you can do today"

Benjamin Franklin

I mentioned in chapter two that the most common time people fail to achieve their goals is the very first step. The longer you delay taking action, the less likely you are to take it. You know how it works—you put something off, you say you will do it tomorrow and something always comes up and eventually it never gets done.

The sooner you do something, the easier it becomes to keep taking action. Realise that there is no perfect time to take action but the time you have—now. What are you waiting for?

When you take action, something amazing happens—you gain this incredible state of mind and an invisible energy called momentum. The scientific theories behind momentum state that once you are moving, it becomes harder to stop and easier to continue. Just like when you make a snowball and roll it down a hill—it gains momentum and before you know it, you have created a boulder!

> *"The most important thing you can do to achieve your goals is to make sure that as soon as you set them, you immediately begin to create momentum. The most important rules that I ever adopted to help me in achieving my goals were those I learned from a very successful man who taught me to first write down the goal, and then to never leave the site of setting a goal without first taking some form of positive action toward its attainment."*
>
> **Anthony Robbins**

Success Formula

One thing that I recommend you do is to create your own success formula. Take all the principles from many of the World's most successful people that I have shared with you and create a structure to work them into your life.

Visualise the sort of attitude you want to have and then commit to acting it out each day.

Create a vision for your life that gets you genuinely excited about living each day.

Flip your thinking around your fears and adopt new empowering beliefs.

Spend time with successful people, master your energy levels and commit to taking the most important actions each day.

Constantly review your goals, visualise your success and talk to yourself like a champion.

Keep taking action, living and learning and eventually you will succeed.

As I said at the beginning of this book, success is not an accident. It is a sequence of steps and when you apply those steps in your life, you will succeed like the many others have before you.

On your marks, get set . . .

GO!

Whatever it is you want to achieve, just make a start today. Even if that start is tiny, the psychological boost you will get from beginning will carry through into the next day and the next and soon enough you will be well on the way to achieving all of your goals.

There is no magic formula for getting started. Unfortunately most people don't start because they are worried about getting it wrong, feeling stupid and being embarrassed. Successful people accept that they won't always have the answers—ever. They accept they may get some things wrong but so what? Who cares if you mess up? Your greatest lessons in life come from your mistakes; don't let fear get in the way of starting. If you ask me—that would be stupid!

What is your very first step?

What could you do right now to get the ball rolling? This instant?

Whatever it is—just do it.

I have chosen the following poem to conclude the book as I think it relays the overall message about living your life with full application.

Martin Robert Hall

Seize the Day

Seize the day, for time is passing,
Seize the day, your days amassing,
Your time to live, and do, and be,
Is now for you a mystery.
To solve each day as it unfolds,
And watch the treasure it beholds.
Now understand your precious time,
Will one day just be over.
And understand the time to live,
Is now, not under clover!
So seize the moment, seize the time,
Seize that precious day.
And fill your life with happiness,
For this is your today!

"Now go to the next chapter if you haven't already started the exercises and get cracking on being the best you can be"

Chapter 6

Bridge the Gap

Nothing happens until something moves"

Einstein

This chapter is designed to get you moving. By completing the exercises in this chapter you will begin to crystallise all of your thoughts and bridge the gap between your thoughts and your actions.

It's time to make it happen.

If you have not yet created yourself a 'focus journal' then write down all the answers to the following exercises in a notepad rather than just on random bits of paper. That way you can keep them all in one place for when you need to come back to them.

Make sure when you complete these exercises that you are in a relaxed environment with no distractions so you can give them your full attention and therefore come up with the most accurate and valuable responses.

Martin Robert Hall

Potential Unlimited *Exercises*

Optimal Response

We covered the importance of establishing a successful attitude in chapter one and how your attitude determines your response to life's events. This is your most powerful resource in leading a successful life.

Complete these exercises and create an attitude that will help you succeed.

Model your heroes

The fastest way to succeed in life is to model successful people.

Think about all the people you admire most in your life. This can include people you know, people you know of and people from history. Why do you admire them? List all the aspects of their attitude that you admire.

Now make a list of all the ways you can come up with to adopt those attitudes in your life.

Create your own advert (1)

At the end of chapter one, there is an advert I have adapted from a campaign by sportswear giant Nike. I have that advert in my focus journal and regularly read over it to give me a boost as it reminds me of having a winning attitude in my life.

If you were to write an advert or a creed that described the sort of winning attitude you want to have in your life, what would it say?

Create your own advert (II)

Start by making notes on all the things you would want it to include and then refine it so it is just the right length to read each day – about one page is right. This is an amazingly powerful way to boost your attitude each day.

You can also print out and include the one I have used if that works for you too. I read it every morning!

Purposeful living

Your attitude in life does not just apply in your career or at home, it applies to everything you do. Your attitude is about how you approach life in general, it is your own unique outlook on life. Your attitude provides purpose behind everything you do, all of your life's activities.

If you were to describe yours in one concise sentence, what would you write?

Consider your role models approach to life, what would you write about them? Now consider what you would want yours to say and capture it in one clear sentence.

Mine is simply 'to inspire and uplift people'. I try to live with this attitude in everything I do whether it is smiling at a stranger walking by, encouraging somebody to go for their dreams, giving an inspirational talk or just making friends laugh.

I hope I have managed to inspire and uplift you with this book.

Capture your favourite qualities in one sentence and then try to approach everything in your life with this attitude.

Open Wide *Exercises*

Creating a vision for your life is one of the most important things you can ever do and is the starting point for achieving everything you want.

Before you can become successful in your life, it is important to have clarity about what success means to you.

What does success mean to you?

What would need to be happening in your life for you to consider yourself truly successful?

It is important to not hold back when completing these exercises and operate from a place of possibility and belief, not from a place of fear. Forget about how you would actually make it happen and all the reasons why you can't for now, just concentrate on answering the questions.

> ### *Ignite Your Imagination*
>
> Remember that your imagination is the creative workshop of your mind. Why would you even have the ability to imagine if it wasn't possible to turn that vision into a reality?
>
> What would you dare to dream for your life if you knew you could not fail?
>
> What would you do if there were no limits?
>
> What could you make your life about to get really excited and inspired?
>
> The best way to answer these questions is to use the same technique that I talked about in *Time for reflection* in chapter four. Write down as many answers as you can, let it all flow out as normally the last few answers are usually the answers you were looking for.

Century Thinking

Write a list of 100 things you would like to do in your life. Yes, 100. No less. Let your imagination run wild. Write down as much as you can think of, no matter how big or how small. Go!

From Imagination to Realisation

Once you have an idea of your ultimate vision for your life, one that will get you excited and inspired beyond belief, the next step is to introduce some deadlines on your dreams. By deadlines, I mean goals. I see goals as 'dreams with deadlines' and they are the bridge from just a dream to making it a reality.

Go through all the answers you wrote down to the previous two exercises and start putting some dates on when you would like to do these things by.

Mark each goal with one of the following;

10 years, 5 years, 3 years, 1 year, 6 months, 3 months, 1 month.

Foreseeable Future (1)

Looking at your vision and the things that get you most excited and inspired in your life;

What would you really like to make the next 5 years of your life about?

Take the things from your vision and slot them onto a timeline of your life. Plot the things you would ideally like to achieve 5 years from now.

Foreseeable Future (II)

What about the next 3 years?

And the next 12 months?

Remember to *Access all areas* and set goals in every area of your life, not just your career which seems to be the most obvious option for everybody. Consider your health, your relationships, fun and enjoyment, your family and personal goals too.

Price it up

Remember in chapter two when we covered paying the price for the things you want – there is always a price. That price comes in personal time, effort and commitment to achieving what you want.

What price will you have to pay to achieve what you want?

Are you willing to pay that price?

If you are not clear on what it will take, do some research and maybe ask some people who have achieved what you want. Then weigh up the costs versus the benefits.

Now decide what you are committed to, write it down and follow through with no excuses.

Get Synced

Now that you are clear on the price you are willing to pay to achieve what you want, the next step is to crystallise that into some specific measures. You do this by setting yourself *performance goals* that reflect the amount of time and effort you are willing to put in and what you believe will be enough to achieve the results you desire.

What will your performance goals be?

Examples might be making a certain number of sales calls each day, exercising for a certain amount of time each day, dedicating a certain amount of time each week to your friends and family.

Map it out

When setting goals, especially big ones, it is very easy to get overwhelmed by the amount of tasks you need to do so breaking your goals down into bite size chunks is essential. Otherwise you will be more prone to making mistakes, feeling overwhelmed and stalling on what needs to be done.

Take each one of your goals and consider all the main actions you will need to complete to achieve each of them. Make a list. Mind-mapping is a great technique for this. See the example below;

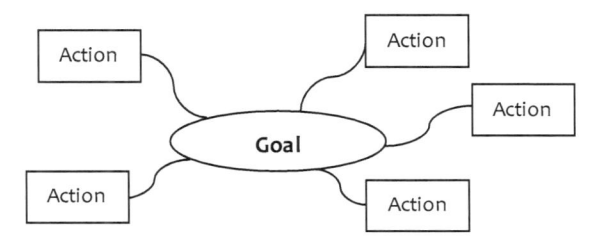

Quantum leap your results

There are two ways to get into a cold swimming pool. One is dip your toe in and confirm your fears about how cold it was going to be. The other is to dive in and start swimming!

When it comes to achieving your goals, you gain more momentum and make much more lasting progress when you take a leap. You may call it a leap of faith.

What would represent a quantum leap for you?

What do you think one of your heroes would do in your situation?

Generate a list of options and then get on with leaping instead of clawing your way to the top.

Limitation Disengage *Exercises*

As we covered in chapter three, nothing gets in the way of optimal performance more than interference in the form of doubt and fear. Successful disengaging and managing these emotions is key to your success.

Make friends with fear

What would you do if you had no fear?

Let your imagination run wild and list down everything that comes to mind. Then go over the list and underline which of these actions would help you achieve your goals.

Fear comes as a result of imagining a negative outcome. Confidence comes from imagining a positive outcome.

What positive spin could you put on each of your fears to change how you feel about it?

For example, if you fear making sales calls the opposite of that may be – I enjoy making sales calls and offering people the opportunity of working with me.

You can come up with as many positive statements for each fear as you like.

Build success filters (1)

How much do you believe in yourself?

Do you believe you are going to succeed? Do you believe you deserve to succeed?

Build success filters (II)

Your beliefs are at the root of all your actions. Ultimately your beliefs are your choice. You choose what to believe and what not to believe.

Think of somebody who you admire greatly, someone who has achieved or is achieving everything you want. What beliefs do you think they have about themselves?

Model similar beliefs about yourself. Write down a list of all the beliefs you will live by from now on.

Your success guarantee

The only way to achieve success is to produce successful behaviour that leads to successful outcomes. It does not matter how you think, what you fear and what you believe unless you show it in the way you act.

You have more control over your behaviour than you do over your emotional state and it is your actions which ultimately determine your results anyway.

What actions are you committed to following through on regardless of how you feel?

Look at some of the things you fear doing, which of those would be the most powerful to follow through on?

How could you make taking these actions easier and more enjoyable?

Realising that successful people don't always feel like taking certain actions is very important. It is taking action regardless of how they feel which separates them from the average person and ultimately guarantees their results.

Optimal Performance
Exercises and strategies

Once you know what you want and have plans of how to accomplish it, the most important thing then is managing yourself and your progress towards your goals. These exercises will help to fast track your success.

Team selection

Write down all the people you spend time with. Consider the following people;

Work colleagues, family and friends.

Now comes the tougher part. Go through this list and put a +/- by their name depending on whether they have a positive (+) or negative (-) impact on you. Don't worry, you don't have to show it to them!

Start spending more time with the people who raise you up and reduce the amount of time you spend with the energy sappers.

Write a list of ways in which you can implement this into your life.

Accountability (1)

Now start thinking about the coaches, mentors and role models you have in your life. These people are crucial for holding you accountable for your actions and reaching your goals.

Do you have a coach, mentor or role model of any kind?

Accountability (11)

If not, who would make the ideal person to help you achieve your goals?

Identify the different forms of support you would like to have;

In your career

In your personal life

Now take some action towards making it happen. These people will propel you towards your goals faster than anyone else.

Optimal conditioning (1)

Apart from the people you spend time with, how else do you plan on positively conditioning yourself for success?

Books

Make a list of all the books you would love to read. The people you would like to learn from and the topics you would like to learn about. Rank your list and then purchase the first book straight away and dip in!

Training Courses

What would be the most useful thing you could learn about right now?

Start researching some courses on these topics. Ask people who have achieved what you want for advice. Do some research on the best courses around and then book yourself on one in the near future. Start outsourcing your success.

Optimal conditioning (II)

Audio Programmes

Identify all the time you have in your week when you could listen to audio. This may be travelling time, whilst exercising, etc. Now make a list of all the things you would love to learn about during this time.

Do some research and see what audio programmes are available on this topic. Pick one and start making some great extra use of your time.

Emotional lock-down (I)

This is one of my many bonus principles I have included only in this section for those of you who made it and it is one that has served me extremely well for many years. Here are several techniques I have used for conditioning myself in my everyday environment;

Audio

Music is one of the most powerful influencers over your mood.

Make a list of all your favourite songs, ones that make you feel great. Now make a song-list or two containing a compilation of these songs. Put the compilation in your car, in your house stereo, on your mp3 player, on your phone, on your computer and every place you listen to music. Take control of your mood and your feel good factor in advance by listening to music that triggers positive emotions in you.

Emotional lock-down (11)

Visual

Use the power of quotes. Print off quotes that inspire you and put them in places where you will see them often. Put them in your home, your car, your office and wherever else you spend time on a regular basis. This technique has helped me become a more relaxed driver, more motivated, happier and more grateful for everything in my life.
Write down your own quotes and lessons you learn from your life and print these off too. This will serve as a powerful reminder of some of your greatest personal lessons.
Collect inspirational pictures. These may be posters of beautiful places you want to visit around the world, places where you have been that bring back positive memories, pictures from your family album, pictures that represent your goals and what your working towards achieving. Dot them about your environment – I use them on my phone, my computer, in my home, my car, my office, my focus journal and even in my wallet!

Actual

Apart from just having positive visual and audio tools, having an object which represents positive attachments is extremely powerful. This could be a piece of jewellery, a stone, a toy, key ring or any item which serves as a strong inspirational reminder.

Optimize your inner genius

Make a list of all the things you love to do. Make a list for work and in your personal life.

Next to each of the items write down why you love to do it.

What is it about it that you love?

Identifying this specifically is key as these represent your internal drivers. Your natural strengths.

What are the things that you do really well?

What activities produce your best results?

Make a list for work and home.

Now think about how you can organise your time so you spend more time focusing on these tasks. Could you delegate more? Could you just cut down on some things? Could you swap with somebody else? Who do you need to speak with to make this happen?

The sooner you start this process, the sooner you get to enjoy yourself more and the more success you will have.

Write down the answers to these questions and then list some ways to integrate these into your life. Put a date on each action and put them in your diary. Job done!

Don't leave this exercise until you have some fixed actions in your diary. No cheating. No excuses. Just do it.

Fuel your performance (1)

Let's have a look at how you can fuel all your energy sources;

Physical energy

What is your diet like? Do you eat healthy most of the time? Do you drink lots of water?

What could you do to make sure you are providing your body with the type of fuel it needs?

There are many options like; learn about healthy eating, hire a personal trainer, buy a book on the topic, ask a friend who is into it.

What about exercise?

Are you getting enough good interrupted sleep each night?

Whatever you need to learn or do to step up these three pillars of physical energy, do it. It is the foundation of your entire being.

Mental Energy

How is your mental energy?

How would you rate your concentration levels?

Is your mind often clear or is it constantly buzzing with activity?

Do you do anything to optimize your mental energy? Do you have regular 'switch off' time?

There are exercises in 'optimize your mindset' for building your mental energy levels.

Fuel your performance (II)

Emotional Energy

Would you say you are mostly in a positive or a negative mood?

Think back over the last two days. Break your days down into segments and recall how you were feeling. Were your emotions generally positive or negative? Do you feel in control of your emotions?

Your emotions will largely be determined by the people you spend time with, whether you have an exciting vision for your life or not and how you condition yourself. If you have completed the exercises on each of these and putting them into practise, then you will be making good progress. There are more exercises in *talk to yourself like a champ* later in this section.

Spiritual Energy

When do you feel most inspired by life?

When do you feel most content?

When do you feel most at peace?

Identify all these times and then start integrating these activities into your life on a daily basis. As I said in chapter four, these activities can just be as simple as reading a good book or having a relaxing bath.

But just because they are simple activities, do not neglect the importance of them. If you need a reminder of their impact, then go back and read the section on *Spiritual Energy* in Chapter Four and the overall impact it has on your performance.

Recharging

We covered the importance of the work-rest ratio.

Now go over your goals and your plans and actions. Look at the next 12 months, the month ahead, the week ahead and even your daily diary. Now apply the work-rest ratio from chapter four to all these timelines. Break your time down into chunks of time which allow you to focus your full presence in the moment and give each goal and individual activity your undivided attention.

60 minutes is a good starting point, moving up to 90/120 minute blocks.

Minimise for maximal output

Apply the law of 'the vital few' widely known as the 80-20 principle which is a super method for maximising your results.

Make a list of your 20 percent activities in each area of your life. Then make a list of your 80 percent activities as it is important to see where you spend your time.

Now make a list of ways in which you can reduce the time you spend on the 80 percent and transfer that time to your 20 percent activities. Revisit this exercise every month and you will rapidly improve every area of your life.

To increase your chances of this happening, schedule a "vital few" review now into your diary for each month for the remainder of the year. Remember – what gets scheduled gets done.

Commit to pledges

Pledges are powerful commitments that are very important to you. They are more important than a promise or a confirmation, they are totally non-negotiable. You do them no matter what because they add amazing value to your life.

Make a list of all the things that add amazing value to your life. Start with one or two and make a pledge for a period of time (minimum 30 days) to following through on these things 100% - no excuses.

Examples may be things like reading, exercise, getting up early, spending quality time with someone, attending something or any one of the principles that you have taken from this book or elsewhere.

Reinforce your efforts

We all love the feeling that comes with a reward. Sometimes the rewarding feeling you get from achieving something is better than the outcome itself.

Make a list of all the rewards you could put in place for achieving certain milestones. Put a balance of rewards in place for both outcome and performance goals and you will constantly have an incentive to keep driving forwards in your life.

Optimize your mindset

We have covered the importance of your mind in this book many times. Even though we all know that our mind is responsible for everything we do, most of us are not taught how to nurture it and keep it in prime shape. The following exercises will help you do just that;

See it to believe it

All great achievers can see exactly what they want before they create it. Visualisation is simply dreaming while you are awake. We do it all the time anyway, even if we are not fully aware of it. Visualisation is just taking conscious control of it.

Writing down a story or creative script of your vision for your life will help to trigger the process. The act of writing something down makes your brain go into its creative zone.

Once you have written it down, read it each day and see it in your mind as if it were happening right now.

There are many books on great visualisation techniques. Explore them. Also, go back and read the section again where I explain how to visualise. Enjoy being day-dreamer!

Clear the fog

When was the last time that your mind totally switched off? I don't mean your body, I mean your mind. The truth is that it never really gets a full rest, not even when were asleep as were busy dreaming!

Meditation is like pressing the stand-by button. You are still awake but your mind is doing the absolute minimum.

Breathing meditation is a great one to kick off with. There are many different meditations. Try sitting down for 10 minutes and not doing anything to start with. Just sit there and count the number of breaths you take. Focus on your breath only, if you lose focus, bring it back immediately and start again. With practise you will improve.

Like anything, you build up your ability to focus a bit at a time. Read up on meditation and integrate it into your life. Your mind probably needs a rest!

Optimize Yourself

Talk to yourself like a champ

As we have discovered, all great achievers talk to themselves like they are already a winner.

Come up with a powerful statement or several that you could repeat to yourself each day. You could even borrow some from others like "I am the greatest"! Once you have at least one, write it down on a piece of card or a post it note and put it somewhere where you will see it all the time. You could even put it in a photo frame on your desk.

Now come up with a statement that you could say to others that does the same. It can be a statement that is made in jest but has positive connotations attached to it – just like "I am the greatest" and "the special one". What would you like others to say about you?

Vital reflections (1)

Quality thinking time is essential or you will forever make bad mistakes.

The key to it is the questions you ask yourself and you have control over them so there is no excuse for poor thinking.

Start by writing a list of 100 questions you would love to know the answers to. Then refine this list it down to your top 10. Answer these.

Many leaders also talk about having one question that you ask yourself consistently, some have a series of three questions that they ask themselves whenever they meet a problem or challenge. Come up with your own favourite question or series of questions.

Examples: What is the lesson here? What can I do to improve things? What is the most valuable use of my time right now?

Vital reflections (11)

Once you have your question, make sure you put it into practise straight away. It is likely that you will adapt, change and improve your questions the more you use them.

Print them out in a template or write them at the front of your diary to serve as a reminder.

Ignite your day

Starting your day with a bang creates an amazing energy you carry with your throughout the day. A poor start to the day does the exact opposite.

What would your perfect start to the day include? Make a list of ideas on how you could spend the first hour of your day to put you in a positive mindset.

This may include exercise, a healthy breakfast, reading an inspirational book, listening to uplifting music whilst getting ready, repeating your positive statement, looking at your goals and visualising your success. Whatever works best for you, just make sure you create a positive routine and follow through on it every day – it will make a huge difference.

I use music, meditation, visualisation, writing and exercise – in that order! And then – BANG I'm on it!

Put all the pieces together

Similar to how you would buy a nice leather case for your favourite CD's to keep them all in one place, creating your own success journal is your way of bringing all the principles you have learnt from this book and everywhere else into one place which you cherish and look at daily.

What would yours include?

Ideas include; your vision for your life, written goals and plans to achieve them, pictures of things you want to achieve, pictures of happy memories, positive statements about your life, a list of all your successes, inspirational quotes, your creed/attitude poem, your list of 100 questions, photocopies of any certificates you have received and anything else you can think of. Get as creative as you like.

Just make it INSPIRING!

My closing comments

Thank you sincerely for taking the time to read my book and invest in your own development. I hope you have taken many valuable lessons and principles from the book that will help you to go on to achieve your dreams in life and be the best you can be.

I am truly grateful to have had this opportunity to share the insights with you that I have learnt from great achievers throughout history and I encourage you to share them with others too.

During my time writing this book many people have asked me how I knew how to write a book and the truth is I didn't know. I just read lots of books from other people and then I started writing this one myself. I didn't get it right first time, in fact I re-wrote parts of it many times and truth be told, it took much longer than expected. But with patience and persistence, I got there in the end. I practised many of the principles included in the book to help me achieve my goal so I know from personal experience that they do work!

I also asked several people for their feedback whilst I was writing the book as I know how important this is. What was surprising was that many of these people who already knew me were very surprised by what I had written and intrigued how I knew so much! I insisted that the only things I know, I have learnt from other people and from personal experience. I don't claim to be anything special by knowing what I know, I have just spent many years studying successful people and working out how they did it.

It is something I have always been interested in and the benefits of that is by understanding how successful people operate and achieve what they want, we can follow a similar path and create the life we want too.

I am sure there are many things you can teach me that I don't know about because you have spent time learning about them. In a conversation with my mum, I said to her that it is no different from the fact she knows lots about beauty and could probably write a book about that. They do say we all have a book in us! (I truly believe that)

So I hope you too now have a good understanding of how to achieve what you want by reading this book and that you go on and practise the principles I have shared with you.

Please don't be one of those people who read a book and then a few weeks later they have returned to all their old ways. Get into action straight away, put the principles to practise in your own life and stay on the path of personal development. Make a commitment to follow through on all the plans you have made as part of reading this book and your life will never be the same again, I promise you that.

And if you are interested in working with me then please contact me at

mrh@martinroberthall.com

or visit my website at

www.martinroberthall.com.

Much love and positive vibes,

Martin Robert Hall.

Recommended Reading

This is a list of all the books that have inspired me, that I have read for the research of my book and that I highly recommend you make part of your reading list to help you achieve greater levels of success and happiness in your life.

Biographies

Dreams from My Father: A Story of Race and Inheritance. Barack Obama

A great read and account from Barack Obama's taking you on a journey of his life through his childhood years to the present day. Much more than just an autobiography.

Fantastic: The Life of Arnold Schwarzenegger. Laurence Leamer

Probably the best account of Arnold Schwarzenegger's life which gives a brilliant insight into the mind of a man who has an obsession for success.

How I play Golf: Tiger Woods

Tiger Woods shares the secrets of his success and his personal experiences and attitudes towards life and the game of golf. Interesting insight into one of the World's most successful sports stars.

Losing My Virginity: The Autobiography. Sir Richard Branson

A great insight into one of the most successful business men in the world.

Managing my Life: Sir Alex Ferguson

Great insight into how Alex Ferguson became one of the best football managers in the world and what helped him develop such a winning mentality.

Mourinho: The True Story. Joel Neto

Very insightful book into the mind of one of the most successful and controversial football coaches in modern day football. Gripping reading.

Muhammad Ali: His Life and Times. Thomas Hauser

Widely considered the best book ever written about Ali. This book provides a brilliant insight into the success of one of sport's all time legends.

No Limits: Michael Phelps

A fascinating insight into the life of the World's most successful Olympian of all time.

Playing For Keeps: Michael Jordan and the World that he Made. David Halberstam

Absolutely compelling reading about the life of one of the greatest sportsmen of all time.

The Second Coming of Steve Jobs: Alan Deutschman

A brilliant look at the life of one of the World's most successful businessmen and who may consider responsible for a technology revolution.

Tao of Jeet Kune Do: Bruce Lee

Brilliant book full of wisdom on Martial Arts and life in general. Packed with philosophy and insights from the mind of a true legend.

Yes Man: Danny Wallace

Really interesting read about Danny Wallace, a guy who changed his life with the use of one word. Funny, interesting and gripping.

Success Manuals

10 Secrets for Success and Inner Peace: Wayne Dyer

A short book of 10 secrets that will do exactly what it says on the cover. A short and powerful read.

80-20 Principle: Richard Koch

In depth book looking at the law of the vital few and full of ways in which we can successfully apply it in our lives.

The Big Leap: Gay Hendricks

Fascinating book about how to break your psychological boundaries and take a leap towards the life of your dreams.

Body Mind Mastery: Dan Millman

Excellent book where East meets West, providing great insights into how we can integrate our body and mind for overall success.

Conscious Living: Gay Hendricks

Great book about living with full awareness every day and tapping into our potential and the potential of the universe. Very insightful.

Do You! Russell Simmons

Brilliant, catchy book with some very powerful lessons by a modern day entrepreneur.

The Four Hour Work Week: Timothy Ferris

If you are interested in becoming more productive with your time and want a book full of tried and tested methods then this is the book for you. A modern day approach to work.

Goals: Brian Tracy

If you want to know everything there is to know about setting and achieving goals, this is the book to read.

How to Think Like Leonardo da Vinci: Michael Gelb

Great book based which simplifies the methods used by Leonardo da Vinci to make him one of the leading thinkers of all time. Great for unleashing your creativity.

How to Win Friends and Influence People: Dale Carnegie

One of the first personal development books I read many years ago. Amazingly simple and powerful strategies for accelerating your success with people.

The IMPACT Code: Nigel Risner

A no-nonsense guide to achieving what you want in life. An easy and enjoyable read.

The Inner Game of Tennis: Tim Gallwey

A 1973 classic book on the psychology of top performers. Still a great read now.

Liquid Thinking: Damian Hughes

A well written book by a great guy who I know personally. Damian captures some valuable lessons from some of the World's most successful people.

The Magic of Thinking Big: David Schwartz

A classic book on personal achievement. Told with great stories that share powerful lessons. A must read.

Mastery: George Leonard

Brilliant book which challenges you to give your best all the time. Packed with wisdom.

Overachievement: John Eliot

Superb book on human performance and full of strategies to up your own game. If you like personal achievement books, you will enjoy this.

The Power of Intention: Wayne Dyer

A deep insight into creating the life you want by one of my favourite spiritual teachers on success.

The Psychology of Winning: Denis Waitley

Old-school methods for succeeding in life by a legend in the industry. Well worth a read.

The Seven Spiritual Laws of Success: Deepak Chopra

Amazingly simple book on creating effortless success in your life.

Strength for Life: Shawn Phillips

Great book which challenges and encourages you to give your best in everything you do.

The Success Principles: Jack Canfield

I class this as the bible of success. A must read for anyone wanting to know the a-z of achieving what you want.

Think and Grow Rich: Napoleon Hill

Considered the all-time classic book on personal achievement. One of my first read and one of my favourites.

Unlimited Power: Anthony Robbins

In depth, detailed guide to achieving unlimited success in your life. Not for the faint hearted, this book is packed with information.

The Winners Bible: Kerry Spackman

Teaches you how to run your brain like a winner and make long lasting changes to the way you think and the way you behave. Packed with useful tools for success.

Bring the power of positive change to your organisation with the . . .

Optimize Yourself Workshops

"Develop a Winning Attitude"

More important than the level of skill, knowledge and ability of your people is their attitude. This is their most important attribute and indicator of how successful they will become. Mastering a winners attitude is at the foundation of all your results and vital to your success. In this workshop you will;

—Master the attitude of a true winner

—Learn how to operate at your best all the time

—Be empowered and take control of your own results

—Come away prepared for any challenge you might face

"Vision and Goal Setting"

Tapping into your creative potential, seeing beyond the present and crystallising your future is your blue print for success. Knowing how to do this effectively is key to achieving everything you want. In this workshop you will;

—Create a compelling vision of your future

—Map out the key steps for the achievement of your goals

—Learn the fastest and most crucial step in achieving your goals

—Accelerate the accomplishment of your goals

"Master a Winning Mindset"

Great achievers in life have what I define as a 'winning mindset'. They master the way they think and how they operate their mind to accomplish great things when others would either fall short or give up. Mastering a similar mindset is crucial if you want to realise all of your ambitions. In this workshop you will;

—Master the feeling of fear

—Become fearless in your thinking

—Adopt the beliefs of a winner

—Master new and successful behaviours

"Optimal Effectiveness"

Once you are clear on what you want and have a compelling vision, how you manage your individual performance determines how successful you become and how fast you achieve what you want. Successful people are effective in doing what needs to be done. In this workshop you will;

—Learn what is key to your success and what is holding you back

—Increase your effectiveness by up to 10 times

—Make the achievement of your goals effortless

—Make better decisions

Martin Robert Hall

Invest in your development and propel your success by bringing the *Optimize Yourself* Workshops to your organisation.

Contact Martin at:	mrh@martinroberthall.com

Or visit:	www.martinroberthall.com

Printed in Great Britain
by Amazon